Making

A Handbook for F   ..asons

Julian Rees

Lewis Masonic

First published 2006

ISBN (10) 0 85318 253 1
ISBN (13) 978 0 85318 253 5

Published by Lewis Masonic

an imprint of Ian Allan Publishing Ltd,
Hersham, Surrey KT12 4RG.
Printed in England by Ian Allan Printing Ltd,
Hersham, Surrey KT12 4RG.

Code: 0606/A2

Visit the Ian Allan Publishing website at
www.lewismasonic.com

Contents

A Note for the Reader   5

The First Degree   7

The Second Degree   55

The Third Degree   89

Suggestions for Further Reading   127

A Note
for the Reader

Freemasonry should be fun. Someone once said: 'If Freemasonry isn't fun, it isn't working'. But on the other hand it is a very serious pursuit, leading us to no less than self-knowledge and self-perfection. This book sets out to resolve that apparent paradox and also to set the enquiring Freemason on his path, whether he is a newly made Freemason or a Freemason of many years' experience and knowledge. This paradox begins with the symbols, so we are going to concentrate on the insight we can gain from a study of them.

Too often, masonic symbols have remained just that — symbols, without a serious commitment on our part to realising their true meaning. They have remained an outward sign, but without the inner meaning. But Freemasonry has no dogma, and does not dictate to us how we should interpret symbols. Since there is no dogma, there seems to be a lack of guidance. Its symbols are mostly allegorical and their meaning hidden. This is not because there is something to hide, far from it, but rather that there is something to be revealed. To discover the true masonic secret, we have to work to bring it forth. It is in the de-coding of the symbols, that the fruits, the insights are gained. There is however a need for a road-map with which to travel the path, a sort of companion on our journey, to hold our hand as we explore for ourselves. This book is intended to work in this way, and to act as a catalyst.

Interpretation of the symbols is not something new for us. It is something that lies inside each one of us, and therefore the challenge is not so much to learn new things, as to remember old ones. In fact, the interpretations of the symbolism of the Craft that we put forward here are certainly not the definitive ones, nor are they exhaustive. They are intended to open the door for you, and to lead you past the frequently given explanations, to enable you to formulate some for yourself. If, for example, the explanation of the significance of the lodge jewels leads you, by contemplation, into unexpected avenues, then follow your own inclination and develop some de-coding of your own. Remember, it is the journey that is important, not the destination.

Since this is a journey, our science is a progressive science. As you probably already know, the path is travelled in three stages, called degrees. Part one of this book is a handbook for the first degree, and for this education of the first degree aspirant to be effective, readers are advised not to stray into parts two and three, unless they are already Fellow Crafts or Master Masons. There are two reasons for this: first, so that your attention is concentrated on the degree in hand, and you can expand your consciousness of that degree before proceeding; second, because the other two parts will not really make sense until you have advanced to those degrees. For the journey to be effective, there is much to be learned and validated at each stage before proceeding to the next. By skipping to a degree higher than the one to which you have been admitted, you would be short-changing yourself. There is plenty to be done here in the first degree before advancing!

As we said, you are embarking on a journey. And there is no hurry. Travel at your own pace. If you feel you need more time with one of the degrees before advancing to the next, tell your proposer or the Master of your lodge that you are not yet ready — they will understand. Above all, have fun!

Enjoy the journey, my Brother.

The First degree

'No man is born into the world, whose work
is not born with him; there is always work,
and tools to work withall, for those who will:
and blessèd are the horny hands of toil!'
James Russell Lowell

It is likely that the first degree in Freemasonry has been recently conferred on you. You may not even have been present at a first degree lodge opening ceremony, and for this reason we will keep that ceremony for later.

You may not have appreciated in detail all that has passed and you may have found the sheer weight of ceremonial overwhelming. We will start at the beginning and take it step by step.

Preparation

Whatever may have been your preparation for Freemasonry, and however much you may have read beforehand, let us begin with your preparation by the Tyler outside the door of the temple. You will remember that your clothing was disarranged, and in an apparently haphazard way, yet in another sense symmetrical. Your right arm, left breast and knee were made bare and your right heel was slipshod. This is the degree of birth, and the baring of parts of the body is emblematic of the helpless state in which we are born.

Think for a moment what intent there might have been in the mind of the Brother preparing you. Think for a moment what effect this might have on an aspirant. After all, you would be unlikely to go about your daily life in this state. You would certainly feel uncomfortable. More than this, you would be unlikely to leave home without money. All this would make you feel fundamentally disoriented. To intensify the disorientation, you were then hoodwinked; you could still feel and hear, but that was all.

This is no idle game. The aim here was, as far as reasonably possible, to shut out the outer world. Even the words of the ritual which you heard in the temple were not those to which you are accustomed in daily life. Freemasonry here sought to shut out the distractions of the material world, and by the words and actions which followed, to concentrate your mind on your inner self, and on the journey on which you have embarked. To step into the temple is to step into another way of being.

Consider this — every part of your body which was made bare is important in the ceremony. Think back for a moment. You right arm was made bare. Your right hand is that with which you make a pledge, either with a handshake, or by making a vow on the Volume of the Sacred Law. It is also the hand with which you demonstrate fidelity. The right arm is made bare to accentuate that. Your left breast was made bare, or more correctly, the symbolism points to baring or opening the heart. An open heart is the most important attribute that could be required of you before your initiation. As you will remember, it was also to your left breast that the poignard was presented — more of this later. Your left knee was made bare because it was on your left knee that you would make your vow. And lastly, your right heel was slipshod. It was necessary, symbolically, to do this, since the lodge is holy ground dedicated to the worship and service of God. This practice accords with that of many religions of removing shoes before entering a place of worship.[1] The lecture puts the preparation of the aspirant in perspective:

'I being neither naked nor clothed, barefoot nor shod, but in an humble, halting, moving posture . . .'[2]

The cable tow about your neck had two symbolic purposes. First, it symbolised the giving up of your freedom prior to initiation. You had submitted to others, placed your trust in them, unconditionally. You can see that you were freely walking into the unknown. You had surrendered yourself to the Brethren, as a mark of humility. This

required a great deal of trust, but by giving up freedom and delivering yourself in this way, you gained an equal amount of freedom. This apparent paradox is explained when you realise that you were gaining freedom from material concerns. For a while, you gave up all other affiliations in order to place yourself completely in the care of others whom you trusted, and achieved a new freedom in so doing.

The cable tow had however another symbolic inference. It would restrain you if you sought to withdraw or hesitate. On the other hand, the poignard presented to your heart prevented you from progressing too quickly. You were thus placed in double jeopardy; by rushing forward you would have been endangering yourself, but holding back would have presented an equal danger. To avoid one danger would have increased the risk of the other. The need for this sort of balance between action and stillness should therefore characterise your masonic journey.[3] To move steadily onwards was your safest course.

Thus you exercised free will in submitting yourself, in order to attain, later, to a greater freeedom. But the most important part of your preparation was undoubtedly being hoodwinked. Material light was withheld to assist you in seeking inner light, or in the words of the lecture 'that my heart might conceive before my eyes should discover'. The intended meaning of material light here, is light as a symbol of opportunity — the opportunity to discover something longed-for, and a desire to leave darkness behind in order to discover the light. It is the emergence of creation out of the darkness of chaos, or of non-creation.

Admission

Once you were prepared, the Tyler knocked on the door; that knock, given on your behalf, heralded the start of your initiation ceremony. He announced you as '. . . a poor candidate in a state of darkness'. The poverty he referred to pointed to your having been divested of so much, but you were also described as poor, because you lacked the richness of spiritual progress. The darkness, as well as being material darkness, was the darkness of un-knowing, the admission that you were in need of light, and was also emblematic of the darkness of the womb before birth. The hoodwink is found in many rites of initiation. As we came out of darkness into light when we were born, so intellectually and spiritually we seek Divine light out of darkness. This search for light goes on at the deepest level, inside each one of us, yet initiation is there to assist that search.

The next part of the Tyler's colloquy contained the phrase 'and now comes, of his own free will and accord'. This is important, since no aspirant should approach such an undertaking in anything other than a willing manner. The Tyler continued: '. . . properly prepared, humbly soliciting to be admitted to the mysteries and privileges of Freemasonry'. Humility was thus advised. Even if, in the popular world, an aspirant was used to carrying on his business or his life in an assertive or even boastful way, he now learns that the opposite is the virtue that will open doors for him. The mysteries of his own nature, and the privileges of self-improvement and spiritual growth that are on offer will be obtained, once again by that subtle blend between perseverance and stillness which we mentioned earlier.

There are however other virtues giving entitlement to those mysteries and privileges, and they were then mentioned:

'*Q.   How does he hope to obtain those privileges?*
A.   By the help of God, being free and of good report.'

By the help of God, being free and of good report. Aspects of freedom, possibly the most important trait in Freemasonry, will come up again and again on your journey. You will remember that, in speaking earlier of freedom, we said that you had voluntarily given up freedom, and in so doing, had gained freedom from material concerns. That now enabled the assistance of God to be invoked, and the approbation of your friends and those who know you. The whole symbolism here is one of testing and of proving. The importance of the Deity in Freemasonry was to become very clear to you soon after your entry into the temple, but the fact that His aid was being invoked at that point is important. From the start then, Divinity was to play a central role in your initiation.

We have talked of freedom, and of Divine assistance, and of the third point — the approbation of your fellows and friends, the 'good report' with which they had recommended you for Freemasonry. As

11

well as having put your trust in the Brethren, they had put their trust in you, and they had done so on the basis of the good opinion in which you were held by your proposer, seconder and other friends you might have in the lodge. A sort of fraternity had already been created between you, your friends and the other Brethren, who were now being asked to place their trust in that judgement. We have here something like a trinity:

the invocation of the assistance of God
your own freedom
your own reputation as reported by others

This is a powerful combination of forces with which to launch you on your journey, but as you can see, it has been carefully crafted; it does not happen by accident.

Here you were then, still in darkness, unsure what would happen next. When the door opened again, you felt a sharp instrument presented to your heart. The poignard has many significations on different levels. In many primitive initiatory rites, painful tests were applied, designed to test the courage of the initiate. This test was to remind you to curb your emotions and to restrain your passions.

At the door of the temple, you were symbolically in great danger. You were, as we mentiond earlier, in a double jeopardy — rushing forward would have been perilous, yet holding back had an equal if opposite danger. It was a crisis point. This point ensured that the start of your initiation would be memorable; you had reached a turning point. Your entrance marked the beginning of your initiation into Freemasonry. This symbolised mystical rebirth, the end of your spirit's descent into matter, and its subseqent return to God, a very critical time, marked by a critical point of danger, which you passed without detriment.

The journey begins

Now you were admitted to the temple and placed in the care of a Brother who was to accompany you during this, your first masonic journey. By now you know that this Brother carried out the office of Junior Deacon, and as your first companion on the journey, you may find that he also becomes a close friend, a sort of reference point for your future masonic career.

Once you had been admitted, the Master addressed you:

'Mr . . . . , as no person can be made a Mason unless he is free and of mature age, I demand of you, are you a free man and of the full age of twenty-one years?'

This question was supremely important. We have mentioned already how important freedom is. Most of us have baggage of some kind, be it social, career or any other kind, a baggage which may weigh us down and may impede our progress. Only the person who is able to be free and unencumbered by any of this, can progress along the path, the person whose compass needle points true north, so to speak. Now you were also asked about your maturity. The age of twenty-one years was until recently the age of maturity, although now of course that has been lowered to eighteen, and aspirants may now be initiated at that age. What Freemasonry requires here is that, to be initiated, a person must be mature, be able to accept responsibility for his decisions and actions, and to have the maturity to accept contrary influences and setbacks with good grace.

Having received this assurance from you, the Master called on you to kneel for the benefit of prayer to the Great Architect. In the prayer, it was proposed that you dedicate and devote your life to the service of God. The Master's supplication to God continued:

'Endue him with a competency of Thy Divine wisdom that, assisted by the secrets of our masonic art, he may the better be enabled to unfold the beauties of true godliness, to the honour and glory of Thy holy name.'

This is a great and defining moment, and is regarded by some as the pivotal point of an initiation ceremony. We speak here of 'unfolding the beauties of true godliness', but we are not yet told how. Unfolding implies that godliness is concealed somewhere, but we are not yet told where. Slowly it dawns on us that, since we are in darkness and our gaze is directed inwards, it is to our own self that this injunction refers — we have no other object to unfold except that which resides within ourselves.

And now, while you were still kneeling, the Master asked you:

'In all cases of difficulty and danger, in whom do you put your trust?'

At this stage, you were aware of the importance of God in this ceremony, and aware that your own relationship with God was very much the centre of what was going on. Even had you not been prompted, the answer was well within your grasp.

By now you will know that you entered the temple from the west, and you were still in the west as the prayer was read. The Master is situated in the east. After the darkness of each night which falls, each new day is born in the east, heralded by the gathering luminosity of the rising sun. The first part of your journey therefore, from west to east, was the beginning of a transit from death to birth, or from unknowing to knowing. But you were to undertake a pilgrimage, with the Deacon, in a clockwise manner, and you may recall that the Master addressed the lodge:

'The Brethren from the north, east, south and west will take notice that Mr . . . . . . is about to pass in view before them, to show that he is the candidate, properly prepared, and a fit and proper person to be made a Mason.'

In other words, you were to follow the path of the sun, to follow the road of life, a circuit followed by many a man in ancient religions on entering a temple.

And so you embarked on your first journey. Although you were under the control of the Deacon, let us remember the essential aspect, for it bears repeating: you embarked on this journey of your own free will. That is the only way in which this journey can be commenced. That is the only way in which it will be a valid journey.

In order to begin, you were told to step off with the left foot. In ancient mythology, the Preserver is always shown crushing the head of the serpent of evil with his left foot. In ancient Egypt, stepping off with the left foot was to step into life.

Trial and approbation

In the schools of the ancient mysteries prolonged periods were allotted to the practical achievement of what is summarised in our first degree. The most severe tests of discipline, purity and self-balance were applied before an aspirant was permitted to go forward.[4] The pilgrimage past the Master in the east and then to the two Wardens, submitting the aspirant to a merely formal trial of suitability, is a vestige of that practice. The lesson for us here is that spiritual consciousness is impossible without purification and trial.

As you approached the Junior Warden, you were about to be tested. In the eighteenth century, the two Wardens were placed either side of the doorway in the west through which you entered. Their function then was as a kind of gatekeeper, to test those who sought entry, and their symbolism in this sense derives from the Roman god Janus. Janus was the god of gates and doors (*ianua*), beginnings and endings, and hence represented with a double-faced head, one face looking in, the other looking out. He was worshipped at the beginning of the harvest time, planting, marriage, birth, and other types of beginnings, especially the beginnings of important events in a person's life. Janus also represents the transition between primitive life and civilization, and the growing to maturity of a young person.

The Junior Deacon by your side assured the Junior Warden that you were, in the words now familiar to you:

'A poor candidate in a state of darkness, who has been well and worthily recommended, regularly proposed and approved in open lodge, and now comes, of his own free will and accord, properly prepared, humbly soliciting to be admitted to the mysteries and privileges of Freemasonry . . .'

and that you hoped to obtain those privileges:

'. . . by the help of God, being free and of good report.'

Only then did the Junior Warden agree to admit you past this, the first obstacle in your progress.

This exchange was repeated at the Senior Warden, the second of the gatekeepers. The repetition served to underline the importance of your qualifications and your suitability, and should have indicated to you the seriousness of your intent, and the intent of those around you. The Senior Warden then presented you to the Master:

'Worshipful Master, I present to you Mr . . . . , a candidate properly prepared to be made a Mason.'

Let us pause here for a moment and review what has happened. First, you came to the lodge, prepared in your heart and in your mind for an uncertain journey, the nature of which was not at all clear to you. Then your physical preparation was undertaken and you were led to the door. Next, the door was opened and you were submitted to the two dangers of impetuosity and cowardice we mentioned earlier. After that, your reliance on God was established, and you were submitted to a symbolic journey accompanied by further trials. So when the Senior Warden presented you to the Master with the words '. . . properly prepared to be made a Mason' the preparation he referred to comprised all of those stages mentioned. Only now were you completely prepared.

You had been symbolically subjected to trials and approbations, but now the Master wanted to assure himself and the Brethren of a six-fold intention on your part. This was a summing up of what had happened so far, a sort of final confirmation that everything was in the right place before proceeding to the more serious parts of initiation. He asked you to declare on your honour:

• that you were not becoming a Freemason against your free will
• that you were not improperly influenced by others to become a Freemason
• that you were not influenced by money or some other base motive
• that your motives had to do with a desire of knowledge and a wish to be of service to mankind
• that you held Freemasonry in high regard
• that Freemasonry could rely on your fidelity

These questions are very searching. A summary might be: you were required to declare, on your honour, that you came seeking knowledge, not because others wanted to you to do so, nor for personal material gain, but because you were prompted from within by a desire of knowledge and a wish to be of service to humanity. There is a hint here that the journey upwards would by no means be easy, and patience, perseverance, caution and courage were needed.

Approaching light

The Master having satisfied himself and the Brethren on these points, the Junior Deacon was to instruct you in the proper means of approaching the Master's pedestal. You will remember that this was achieved by three steps, the first one short, and the other two increasing in length, your heels always in the form of a square. The symbolism of the three steps is that, although we embark on our journey with reticence and uncertainty, as we progress, we gain in confidence and our integrity is, little by little, proven to ourselves.

There is a further symbolism of your journey so far, and one that again touches on freedom. The aspirant for Freemasonry should have begun to desire more than material things; he should have freed himself from them, in the desire for knowledge and growth, and so has become free in that sense. This is recognised as you passed the Junior Warden, representing man's material nature, and the Senior Warden, representing the soul. Having passed the Senior Warden, you then approached the Master, emblematic of the Divine Spirit, and called on him symbolically to give you light. That is the true nature of your ever-advancing journey towards the Master, symbolically the source of light and Divinity.

Once you had arrived at the pedestal, the Master emphasised once again to you that Freemasonry:

'. . . requires a perfect freedom of inclination in every candidate for its mysteries. It is founded on the purest principles of piety and virtue . . .'

and in order to secure those privileges, a vow of fidelity was required. You affirmed that you were willing to take that vow. But what is the essential nature of the vow that you took? The Master assured you that

17

there was nothing in the vow which would conflict with your duties elsewhere, either civil, moral or religious. Although the words of the vow were couched in rather archaic language, their import is a direct and simple one — join with us, in a vow of faithfulness to morality, in the shape of brotherly love, relief and truth.

Freemasonry is more than the physical organisation which the outside world perceives. Here, there are no secrets to preserve; practically everything about Freemasonry, on the physical plane, has already been published. The masonic pursuit is not secret, but rather very personal.[5] In this sense, secrets are not something to be concealed, rather to be contained. An artist who creates does not reveal his creation before it is complete, as to do so would drain the energy from it. In addition to this, for an aspirant to reveal too much would harm the progress of those aspirants who come after him. You therefore pledged yourself to talk about the secrets and mysteries of Freemasonry only to those Freemasons who are on the same level as you. To do otherwise, it was implied, would lead you to sever yourself from spiritual progress.

Think now for a moment about the sequence of events. The vow you took came immediately before the restoration of light. It was as though that vow summed up all the tests and trials, and that only now could the Master and Brethren decide that you could be trusted with more light. And the words of the Master at this point were yet one more milestone on your journey away from darkness:

'Having been kept for a considerable time in a state of darkness, what, in your present situation, is the predominant wish of your heart?'

for it is to your heart, here as elsewhere, that the greatest appeal was being made. We cannot overstate the importance of the heart in our masonic quest. In most religious and philosophic traditions there is a current theme which associates the spiritual thinking process with the heart rather than with the mind. This suggests that we think with our brains, but we intuit with our hearts. A prayer well known to many of us exhorts God to 'cleanse the thoughts of our hearts by the inspiration of Thy Holy Spirit', so the heart here is made an instrument, not of the body, but of the spirit.

The answer was once again well within your grasp without the need of prompting, and the Master spoke the words:

'Let that blessing be restored to the candidate.'

Knowledge through light

This must be one of the most important moments in Freemasonry, so rich is it with meaning and revelation. Each soul is part of the Divine whole and cannot be separated from it. You had just emerged from the darkness of materialism, seeking Divine light, which is within you. The intended meaning of light here is light as a symbol of opportunity — the opportunity to discover something longed-for, and a desire to emerge from the darkness of materialism and ignorance. It is the emergence of creation out of the darkness of chaos, or of non-creation. And the first things you discovered were three symbolic sources of light. There, on the Master's pedestal, were the three elements which would be the most potent in your search: the Volume of the Sacred Law, the square and compasses. The first of these 'great lights', the sacred writings, is Divine inspiration, since the Sacred Volume contains God's will revealed to man. Without the Divine spark, which speaks from the innermost recesses of the soul, we shall remain in darkness all our life. The second, the square, is that symbol which helps us to act in our lives in a measured way. The compasses remind us that we are an integral part of mankind. So when the Master says 'Let that blessing be restored to the candidate', we recognise light as a blessing in more than the material sense. A synonym of 'blessing' is 'grace'. Grace, as emanating from God, is clearly in evidence in this most important part of your initiation ceremony.

After a suitable pause to allow for the momentous nature of what had just passed, the Master's next words to you were:

'Rise, newly obligated Brother among Masons.'

This was truly the summit, the climax of your initiation, and the character of the ceremony changed markedly at this point.

19

The second part of the ceremony was subsidiary to the first, but it became in a sense more serious, in that you now needed to apply your consciousness to the many explanations, evolutions and revelations taking place. Doubtless the three great lights would remain in your mind and heart as a touchstone of your new profession, and around them would revolve all that would now be explained to you.

First there were the three lesser lights:

'. . . situated east, south and west, [which] are meant to represent the sun [in the south], moon [in the west] and Master of the lodge [in the east]; the sun to rule the day, the moon to govern the night and the Master to rule and direct his lodge.'

You may remember that there was a pillar at the Master's pedestal in the east, comprising the Ionic order of architecture, one at the Senior Warden's pedestal in the west, comprising the Doric order, and one at the Junior Warden's pedestal in the south, comprising the Corinthian order. These then are emblematic of the lesser lights, and also of the three great pillars which are set to support a Freemason's lodge. In that further sense they represent wisdom, strength and beauty. So here, as in many cases, we have layers of symbolism laid one on the other, and exploration of these layers by the new aspiring Freemason can prove fascinating and satisfying.

The three principal officers of the lodge

This is a good place to pause and to think for a moment about the symbolic meaning of the three principal officers of the lodge — the Master and the two Wardens. The Master, as we have heard, represents the sun to rule the day. As God the creator called the world out of nothing, so the Master calls the lodge into being each time he opens it. He is placed in the east, the place of light; as the sun rises in the east to dispense light and life to humankind on earth, so the Master dispenses light and instruction to the Brethren of his lodge. But he has in truth a dual function; he also represents the Divine spark, which speaks to the spirit within us, ever striving for the light, never separated from the Divine source of its being. The Master therefore assists us on our journey towards perfection, and may therefore be described in this context as the spirit.

The Senior Warden represents the setting sun, and thus the transformative aspects of the Deity. As the Master is placed in the east to remind us of the light of life, so the Senior Warden is in the west, to remind us of the onset of night and, ultimately, of death. For this reason, the jewel on the Senior Warden's collar is the level, to signify that death, the great leveller, will reduce us all to the same state. In the nature of man, he represents the soul, the vessel linking our lower and higher states of being.

The Junior Warden represents the sun at its meridian. He stands for the way of life, the journey between birth and death. In the nature of man, he stands for the self; as we have seen, the other two principal officers stand for the soul and the Divine Spirit.

This symbolism has a parallel with the three steps you took on approaching the Master's pedestal. The first step, short and hesitant, may be likened to the body, the material self, searching for its spirit, for spiritual progress. The second step, not quite so hesitant, was taken on behalf of the soul, dimly aware of the spiritual dimension. The third step, while still in darkness, was more sure, and knew that the spiritual goal, unity with God, was within reach, and did not need material light to know that.

In every degree in Freemasonry, these three principal officers work together to advance the aspirant. So it is also in the spiritual life, for self, soul and spirit must work together if real progress is to be made.

Explanations and revealing

The Master then reviewed the dangers we examined earlier and informed you that:

'. . . all squares, levels and perpendiculars are true and proper signs to know a Mason by.'

We will examine those geometrical forms later, for their own symbolism, but for now you were required to:

'. . . stand perfectly erect, your feet formed in a square, your body *being thus considered an emblem of your mind, and your feet of the rectitude of your actions.'*

Later on we will be speaking about the tracing board and the circle bounded by two parallel lines. The tracing board lecture has this to say:

'In all regular, well-formed, constituted lodges there is a point within a circle round which the Brethren cannot err . . .'

The symbolism of standing erect is very important; it implies that by this stance you can be at your own centre, a 'place from which you cannot err'. It also means that your body forms a square with the ground. More importantly, you are an emblem of the conduit from earth to heaven, linking Man to God, another allegory that we will explore later when considering the plumb rule, an emblem of uprightness and truth, and Jacob's ladder, another conduit giving access to God. 'Your feet formed in a square.' You took the first regular step in Freemasonry, a step in which your feet came naturally into the form of a tau, or T-shaped cross, which is the emblem of generation or creation. As the first regular step in Freemasonry, it also implies that our natural and animal passions must be trod underfoot and brought under control, otherwise we can make no progress in our building, nor can we advance towards a true knowledge of God.

The sign, token and word which were then communicated are in reality not secrets. They are modes of recognition, each one with its own symbolism, but we do not reveal them to the outside world for the reasons we mentioned in regard to symbolism; namely, to do so would devalue them and dissipate their energy and the energy that you will need on your journey. To reveal them would also compromise their value for those aspirants who follow. But the actual sign, token and word are in reality an allegory. You will find, on your masonic journey, that Fellow Freemasons are often easy to recognise, not by those externals, but by the persona that they project in their lives, so that those symbols are an allegory for the spiritual progress that has taken place in the individual.

A new journey

A new journey now began for you, one where you would again be tested, but this time you had a good idea of the answers to give. More than this, you were now a Brother among Freemasons; there was no longer a need to test your fidelity, or to test your motives, as there had been previously. This second journey, after enlightenment, was a rehearsal for tests of your fidelity that might come in the future, a means of preparing you to leave the lodge to go once more into the outside world. But this new journey also symbolised that the Wardens, whom we can now recognise as the self and the soul, were testing your new-found spiritual dimension.

The journey was interrupted at the Senior Warden's pedestal; he addressed the Master:

> *'Worshipful Master, I present to you Brother . . . . . . on his initiation, for some mark of your favour.'*

The key word here was 'mark'. In yourself, you were already marked by your progress, marked as a person who had commenced the masonic journey, and who was close to completion of the first stage. But now, you were to be marked outwardly, as proof to others of the new state you were in. The Master directed that you should be invested with 'the distinguishing badge of a Mason', the plain white lambskin apron. Note that the Master did not invest you himself; the Senior Warden (soul) called on the Master (spirit), but was told that it was the soul which must invest the regenerated person with that outward sign of the change he had undergone. It is therefore the Senior Warden who set the seal on your initiation. You were now marked as an Entered Apprentice Freemason.

After investing you, the Senior Warden referred to the antiquity of the apron, a badge which also implies the dignity of honest labour. He referred to the apron as:

> *'. . . the badge of innocence and the bond of friendship . . .'*

two important attributes, which you should always remember. Innocence relates not so much to a quality free from guilt, but to the state we are in when we are born, untainted by the adverse currents of life. Friendship brings us once more to mutuality, and to the notion that together we are stronger than the sum of our individual strengths. In one of the very old constitutions of Freemasonry, we read the words:

'For human society cannot subsist without concord, and the maintenance of mutual good offices; for, like the working of an arch of stone, it would fall to the ground provided one piece did not properly support another.'

The Master made it clear that this badge is in a sense your passport to a lodge of love and harmony. As such, it was not to be worn, nor should you enter a lodge, if there was a chance that love and harmony would be compromised by any differences you might have with another Brother in that lodge. The mere presence of two Brethren who are at variance with each other, would disturb the atmosphere. This is a purely spiritual atmosphere, which will be disturbed even if the disagreement is not an open one, and a hidden disagreement can still be detected by sensitive individuals.

A new test and new symbols

You were then placed at the north-east part of the lodge, and your feet were once again positioned in the form of a square, an emblem now well known to you. The north-east corner of a building is that point where the foundation stone, the corner stone, is traditionally laid. It is interesting to note why that particular point of the compass is chosen. Traditionally, in the northern hemisphere, the north is the place of darkness, and the sun, the glory of the Lord, rises in the east, but crosses the heavens east to west across the southern part of the sky. Being placed at the north east corner thus symbolises your progress from darkness to light. The light of day is essential for every builder, but it is important to remember that you are building your own temple — a spiritual temple to the glory of God, and you are no less in need of figurative light.

In this situation, the Master was about to test your principles. Here, you were about to start your labours, at the lowest level so to speak, and everything depended on your response. You were

24

required to give proof of your state of poverty, but now you had made the connection between material and spiritual poverty, so in affirming that you had no means to dispense charity, you were doubly blessed! This test would probably remind you for the rest of your life of the virtue of charity, material as well as spiritual. Genuinely remarkable benefit has resulted from this section of ritual, both within Freemasonry and outside it.[6] A demand for charity, therefore, also required that you committed yourself to a continuation of the progress within yourself, by dint of hard work and Divine grace.

The conclusion of the main part of the initiation ceremony was the presentation and explanation of the working tools of the degree, which you will remember were the twenty-four inch gauge, the common gavel and chisel. These working tools appear to be mechanical instruments, yet they provide us with valuable insights. Let us review the words of the presentation:

'The twenty-four inch gauge is to measure our work, the common gavel to knock off all excrescences, and the chisel to further smooth and prepare the stone, and render it fit for the hands of the more expert workman.'

After presenting the tools, the Master explained that it is our custom to regard them as figurative tools and to apply them to our morals. In this sense, he said:

'the twenty-four inch gauge represents the twenty-four hours of the day –
• part to be spent in prayer to Almighty God
• part in labour and refreshment
• part in serving a friend or Brother in time of need . . .'

You will recall two objects in the lodge; the rough ashlar and the perfect ashlar. The rough ashlar is a rough stone on the Junior Warden's pedestal, in the form of a more or less regular cube, but rough-hewn. The perfect ashlar is a stone in the form of a perfect cube, smooth to the touch, and suspended from a derrick, by means of a metal cramp called a lewis. This arrangement is placed on the

Senior Warden's pedestal. These then are the stones to which the working tools indirectly refer — the one rough-hewn, pointing to the work expected of the apprentice, and the other representing what might be achieved by skill and experience. The working tools are the implements used on the rough ashlar to transform it into a perfect ashlar. If we think for a moment about these tools, we will realise that they are not tools used in construction at all — they are in fact the tools used in preparing the materials prior to construction.[7] So it is also in the speculative or figurative sense — they are emblematically the means we use to prepare our own character for the continuing building work — the erection of our own inner temple. The gavel represents the driving force, a force used on the chisel, which is a much finer tool and capable of much more subtle, analytical work. The twenty-four inch gauge, on the face of it, is completely inert, yet it acts in a crucial way, to ensure that our acts and their consequences are measured, in every sense of that word.

The main part of the initiation ceremony was now over, and the Master permitted you to restore yourself, before the summing-up, or charge after initiation.

A charge

On the face of it, there seems little point in here reiterating the words of the charge. They seem to be self-explanatory. Yet the wealth of information and instruction may be intimidating. Let us see if we can tease out a summary which will be more instantly memorable.

Freemasonry is ancient and honourable. We do not know for certain how long it has existed, but the precepts of masonic morality are so universal, that mankind must have been practising them since the dawn of time. And it is easy to see that the virtue of honour naturally accrues to such a society through that very practice of morality, what is summed up in the words 'every moral and social virtue'.

The Volume of the Sacred Law is central to our masonic profession. By it you will be taught:

'. . . the important duties you owe to God, to your neighbour, and to yourself.'

26

This trinity has echoes of the three great lights in Freemasonry, the Volume of the Sacred Law, the square and compasses, since the sacred volume itself, being God's revealed will to mankind, is the vessel, containing those duties we owe to Him. You will remember that the square regulates our lives and actions, and its symbolism reminds us of the duties we owe to ourselves, to develop our moral character. The compasses are to keep us in due bounds with all mankind, and hence remind us of the duties we owe to our neighbour.

The next two sections of the charge deal with our duties as a citizen of the world, and with our conduct in public and in private. Here we deal with the importance of a correct attitude towards authority and the law, and we underline that, if a correct moral conduct is required of us in our personal dealings, then that is no less important in our dealings towards the world at large and towards the state. Four virtues are recommended, called the cardinal virtues, of temperance, fortitude, prudence and justice.[8] We will speak about these in the section devoted to the ornaments, furniture and jewels of the lodge.

Virtues of secrecy, fidelity and obedience are recommended. We touched on secrecy — on the need, not to conceal, but rather to contain the elements with which we are working on our personal journey. Fidelity is that which binds us to world-wide Freemasonry and to its constitutions and landmarks, in the form of the sign, token and word, as we mentioned earlier, and to take care about whom we recommend into the Craft. And in conclusion, we are urged to study such of the liberal arts and sciences as may lie within the compass of our attainment. This seems unexpected. In fact, they form an important part of the second degree, so the Master, by introducing them at this point, right at the end of the first degree, is in a sense directing us towards work we might well undertake to prepare ourselves for the next stage. In Freemasonry, as elsewhere, these seven liberal arts and sciences are known by the names of grammar, rhetoric, logic, arithmetic, geometry, music and astronomy.

The lodge as a holy place

You may have noticed the presence in the temple of an object we call

27

the tracing board. In some lodges, this board is placed in the centre of the temple floor. In others, it stands against the Junior Warden's pedestal in the south. On it are depicted many masonic symbols. In most lodges, an explanation of the tracing board is not given at this point. In fact, that explanation forms part of the first lecture[9] and so we will now delve into the fuller symbolism contained there. Early accounts of the consecration of a new lodge refer to the presence of '. . . the lodge, which is placed in the centre, covered with white satin . . .'[10] It is clear that this 'lodge' referred to a pictorial representation of symbols, and was in real terms a symbolical lodge. The lodge is described as being of infinite dimension:

'. . . in length from east to west, in breadth between north and south, in depth from the surface of the earth to the centre, and even as high as the heavens.'

But the lodge is a model of the human psyche. 'In depth from the surface of the earth to the centre.' This points out the distance between the superficial consciousness of our untutored mentality, and what may be the Divine consciousness possible at the centre of our being. 'Even as high as the heavens' clearly indicates that we may, with perseverance, develop our potentialities to the full.[11]

Our lodges stand on holy ground, and three offerings are given as the reason. The first was Abraham's willingness to sacrifice his own son when God called on him to do so. The second offering comprises the prayers offered by King David to appease God's anger. The third offering comprises the thanksgivings made by King Solomon to God at the completion of the first temple at Jerusalem. But for us, the real truth of that statement may be that the ground of our lodges is hallowed by the work of Brethren in the lodge over the course of many years.

Our lodges are symbolically situated due east and west, because all places of worship to God ought to be so. In the masonic sense there are three reasons for this. First, that the sun rises in the east and sets in the west. Secondly, because learning originated in the east and spread to the west. The third reason concerns the orientation of King Solomon's Temple. When the Israelites were released from slavery in Egypt, Moses, under the command of God, erected a tent or tabernacle in the wilderness. God commanded that this tabernacle should be situated

28

due east and west, and it was this ground plan which Solomon later copied in the construction of the temple at Jerusalem.

Wisdom, strength and beauty

Symbolically, our lodges are supported by three pillars, called wisdom, strength and beauty: wisdom to contrive, strength to support and beauty to adorn. These three pillars are the most prominent feature of the tracing board. Wisdom is twofold: it is that which invokes a deep understanding as a counterpoint to wide information, but it is also a capacity for sound judgement, and it is easy to see how the two may work in harmony. We need wisdom to conduct us in all that we do, and it is for wisdom that we strive throughout our masonic journey. In that striving, we will count on the support, not least of the Brethren around us, who lend us strength, the strength of mutuality, hence the second of the three pillars. The symbolism here is that our common strength is greater than the sum of its several parts. Beauty is to adorn, but we speak here not of the beauty of outward form. So often in the world around us, beauty of form or of expression are held in high regard, yet for the aspirant in Freemasonry, beauty refers to that which is evolving, growing and maturing inside himself. Inner beauty, or harmony and peace, are those fruits that may be ours on our journey.

These three pillars, we are told, are emblematic of Divine attributes. They further represent Solomon, for his wisdom in constructing the Temple; Hiram, King of Tyre, for his strength in supporting him; and Hiram Abiff, the artist who beautified and adorned the temple. You will recognise these pillars in the lodge; they are those we referred to earlier as the three lesser lights, the Ionic column placed by the Master, the Doric column by the Senior Warden and the Corinthian column by the Junior Warden.

Heaven and earth

The covering of a Freemason's lodge is 'a celestial canopy of divers colours, even the heavens'. On the first degree tracing board you will see seven stars, emblematic of that celestial covering. The philosopher Immanuel Kant once said:

'Two things fill the mind with ever-new and ever-increasing wonder and awe: the starry heavens above me and the moral law within me.'

By linking those two in that way, he encapsulated that which demonstrates, for Freemasons, the infinity and beauty to which our morality aspires.

One of our routes towards the goal of celestial perfection, even if we do not fully arrive there, is by Jacob's ladder. On the tracing board the lower end rests on the Volume of the Sacred Law, and at its summit is a blazing star representing God. The symbolism of this derives from the biblical legend, in which Jacob fraudulently obtained the blessing of his father Isaac, the blessing which was the birthright of his brother Esau. When Jacob's crime became apparent, he was threatened with death by his brother, and was obliged to flee. Stranded in the hostile desert, he lay down to sleep, with no covering other than the canopy of heaven. As he slept, he had a dream in which he saw a ladder reaching from earth to heaven, with angels ascending and descending on it. Jacob was so impressed with this vision, that when he awoke, he declared that the spot on which he lay was the house of God, and the ladder was the gate of heaven.

The angels ascending and descending the ladder represent those aspiring to Divine grace, and those bringing down God's blessing to man. They are carriers between the heavenly and earthly realms, passing upwards with petitions, downwards with grace and salvation. The ladder is composed, as you would imagine, of many rungs. The three principal ones are named Faith, Hope and Charity, depicted on the tracing board by three figures: one female (Faith) and the other two, angelic figures. Faith is of course important. It is the gateway to belief in God. It is the evidence of things not seen; it is the substance of those things we aspire to spiritually. Hope speaks to us of the constancy of God's care for us, even in times of pain and distress. Charity is, like all bright jewels, a multi-faceted ornament. It does of course speak to us of our responsibility towards those less fortunate than ourselves, but it also transcends the material, and is the catalyst enabling us to know and to love the world at large: a religion of harmony, harmony in ourselves and through that, harmony with others. The ladder on this tracing board rests on the

Volume of the Sacred Law; thus adherence to the Divine law is the gateway to heaven.

This ladder represents a union of celestial and terrestrial domains, and therefore the oneness of God and man. Another symbol of this union is Solomon's seal, the hexalpha, resembling a six-pointed star, formed by inverting one triangle on top of another and interlacing them. Thus we have one triangle pointing to heaven, the other pointing to earth, but being interlaced, they are inextricable, as God's nature is inseparably that of man.

The Rule of Three

Many times in Freemasonry we will come across groups of three, trinities or triptychs, and here what we call the Rule of Three comes into operation. Where we have an active function and a passive function, there is a third which serves to promote and maintain a balance between the other two. An example of this is the working tools. The gavel is an example of the active principle. It delivers the blows on the stone or on the chisel. This represents man's passionate or driving nature. The chisel, the passive principle, receives the blows of the gavel, but is in itself a very sharp and refined instrument, superficial but not trivial, with a potential for very fine and detailed work, and full of analytical potential. This represents man's ability to analyse, classify and communicate. The twenty-four inch gauge is the balancing, measuring principle and mediates between the other two. It may control the active principle, and stimulate the passive, in order to promote a balance, or to ensure a measured approach.[12]

Ornaments

Now we come to three new triads, each of which obeys the Rule of Three: the ornaments, furniture and jewels of the lodge. The ornaments are the mosaic pavement, also called the square pavement, the blazing star and the tesselated border round the mosaic pavement. The mosaic pavement is the black and white chequered floor, pointing out the diversity of objects in the creation. There is no more stark contrast to our senses than black and white,

31

darkness and light, evil and good, tragedy and happiness, even death and life. The floor is in truth an emblem of our passage through our earthly existence, composed as it often is of darkness and light. The blazing star reminds us of 'the omnipresence of the Almighty, overshadowing us with His Divine love and dispensing His blessings amongst us; and by being placed in the centre it ought to remind us that, wherever or however assembled, God, the overseeing eye of providence, is always in the midst of us, overseeing all our actions and observing the secret intents and movements of our hearts'.[13] The tesselated border round the mosaic pavement or carpet in the temple, is that which binds the other two together, emphasising the unity of the whole, the Divine world and the terrestrial, united. In the same way, you will notice that the tesselated border is the border of the tracing board itself, binding all the symbols together.

Furniture and jewels

The furniture of the lodge is composed of our next triad: the Volume of the Sacred Law, the compasses and square, and are of course the three great lights in Freemasonry, which we have already visited. We are again reminded of our union with, and obligation to, God, our fellow men, and ourselves, and you will see that these three provide a constant reminder of the importance of their symbolism.

The jewels of the lodge are not one triad, but two; the movable jewels and the immovable jewels. The movable jewels are the square, level and plumb rule. After light had been restored to you, the Master told you that

'. . . *all squares, levels and perpendiculars are true and proper signs to know a Mason by.*'

These three jewels are shown on the tracing board, either resting against the bases of the three pillars, or as a group in the foreground. These are called movable, because they are the jewels worn by the Master, Senior Warden and Junior Warden on their collars, and are passed on when those Brethren relinquish those offices to other Brethren. When we considered the working tools earlier, we made reference to the nature and appearance of the two ashlars, the rough ashlar on the Junior Warden's pedestal and the perfect ashlar on that of the Senior Warden. We said then that these were the stones to which the working tools indirectly refer — the one rough-hewn, representing the work of the apprentice, and the other representing what might be achieved by skill and experience. The square is that implement with which we test the perfect ashlar, to ensure that it has been properly worked by the experienced Mason. As the Master's jewel, it is therefore that emblem denoting the square conduct of the Master required when ruling and governing the lodge. The level, the Senior Warden's jewel, is that denoting equality. It demonstrates that when we are born, we are all equal and that when we die, our only distinctions will be those of goodness and virtue. The Senior Warden therefore is required to exercise his duties with a sense of equality towards all. The plumb rule is a reminder of Jacob's ladder, in that it too connects heaven and earth. As an upright emblem, it speaks to us of rectitude and of truth.[14] It seems to tell us that, if we can keep our personal gyroscope upright and not be blown over by influences that may be contrary in our lives; if we can avoid malice and revenge, if we can temper our passions, and steer a course between excess and deficiency and not let self-interest stand in the way of correct action, then great spiritual rewards can be ours.

The immovable jewels are the tracing board itself, the rough ashlar and the perfect ashlar. They are called immovable because they lie open in the lodge for the Brethren to moralise on. In times past, in place of a tracing board, the Brethren drew designs of symbols on the floor, in the course of the lodge meeting, in order to study them and discuss them, and draw out the inner meaning of the symbols. This then became codified in the form of permanent cloths or boards, one for each degree, sometimes called 'floorings', or 'floor cloths'.[15] The rough ashlar is clearly visible, near to the base of the Corinthian (Junior Warden's) pillar, and the perfect ashlar, supported by the derrick, is near to the Doric (Senior Warden's) pillar.

Before we leave the ashlars, let us for a moment consider the new Entered Apprentice as an allegory of the rough ashlar. A very wise commentator[16] sums up this aspect as follows: humanity is like a quarry from which stone is to be cut to construct a temple to God. Many parts of this quarry will be hewn out to make the building. As long as the rock remains in the quarry, it is part of the mass and experiences what the mass experiences. The Entered Apprentice is about to be separated from the mass, and to undertake to live his life as an individual, as a separate stone. It is a step which only he can take, and he can take it only for himself. Once he is separated from the mass, like the rough ashlar which will never again be part of the quarry, the Entered Apprentice can never go back. Put in another way, once he has had an insight into his nature and realised the Divinity inside himself, he can never un-know that part of his nature. He will now be an individual, with individual responsibilities, for the rest of his life.

More about the tracing board

If you look at the front of the altar on the tracing board, you will see a circle between two parallel lines. Since the top of the circle is also the top of the altar, the Volume of the Sacred Law rests on the circle. This is referred to in the lecture:

'*In all regular, well-formed, constituted lodges there is a point within a circle round which the Brethren cannot err. This circle is bounded between north and south by two grand parallel lines, one representing Moses, and the other King Solomon . . . In going round this circle, we must necessarily touch on both those parallel lines, likewise on the Sacred Volume, and while a Mason keeps himself thus circumscribed, he cannot err.*'[17]

The parallel lines symbolise Moses receiving Divine law from God on the one hand, and King Solomon dispensing Divine law to mankind on the other. American rituals state that these parallel lines refer to the two Saints John, St. John the Baptist, whose feast is at midsummer, and St. John the Evangelist, whose feast is at midwinter, and this tradition dates from the time that the Craft was essentially christian in content. The symbolism of the circle is that of the individual finding his way to the centre of his being, and finding the Divine spark within him.

And finally, the corners of the tracing board have tassels appended to them, meant to remind us of the four cardinal virtues: prudence, fortitude (also known as courage), temperance and justice. A person is:

- prudent, when knowledge of how to live (wisdom) informs his reason
- courageous, when informed reason governs his capacity for anger
- temperate, when it also governs his appetites
- just, when each part performs its proper task with informed reason in control.

Notice the predominance of 'informed reason' here. This is why justice and uprightness are often linked. The justness mentioned takes us back to the subject of the plumb rule, a symbol of uprightness and of truth.

Before we move on, there is one important aspect of Freemasonry in the first degree which has not been touched on: the three grand principles on which Freemasonry is founded. These are brotherly love, relief and truth, and curiously they are not mentioned in the ceremony of initiation. We mentioned at the beginning that the unveiling or revealing of the meaning of symbols was important. Since these three grand principles are not mentioned in the initiation ceremony itself, nor are they depicted on the tracing board, we are free to search them out amongst the symbols we have so far. Brotherly love is the foundation not only of Freemasonry, but of a harmonious society. We have been born not only to care for ourselves, but for the aid, support and protection of each other. Brotherly love unites people of every country, sect and opinion. The second grand principle, relief, flows from the first, since relief from distress and suffering has a tendency to bind together the fortunate and the less fortunate in any society, and a lack of care will only lead to divisiveness. Truth, the third grand principle, is the one which co-ordinates and binds the first two. It combines fidelity, loyalty and constancy, but also indicates for us correctness of morals, and is closely allied to the third movable jewel, the plumb rule, an emblem of uprightness.

A summary

You may well be forgiven for viewing what has passed as an epic journey! It has certainly been a journey full of insight, but perhaps overwhelming, and it has all taken place in a relatively short time. For an aspirant to Freemasonry, the advantage of setting out the ceremony of initiation and the symbols of the first degree in the way we have done, is that it affords him time; time to explore, time to stop and go back, if needs be, and to make coherent sense of the whole. Let us try to sum up now what has passed.

An aspirant places his trust in the Brethren of the lodge. They place their trust in him. He is prepared, physically and mentally, for a journey of discovery, a discovery that will take place mostly within himself, and for this reason he is hoodwinked. This preparation requires that he is disoriented in order to forget, as far as possible, his material surroundings, so as to remember some truths within himself. He is tested and approved, and finds his relationship with Divinity. Then he makes a pledge and light is restored to him, material as well as inner light.

The light he first sees on being restored is composed of the three great lights in Freemasonry. He then discovers symbols and has some insight into what they may mean, and this is expanded during his subsequent new journey. He learns of the importance of the three principal officers in the lodge, as well as the nature and importance of secrets. He is invested with the badge of an Entered Apprentice Freemason and is symbolically set as a corner stone of the building. His earthly and spiritual poverty are established, and the tools with which he might prepare the symbolic stones for his building are presented to him. Following this, his duties are outlined: duties to God, to his fellow men, to himself, to society, to the State, and to Freemasonry in particular. And lastly, we have studied the symbolic structure and content of the lodge.

It has been quite a journey, and it is not over yet, since now your own input is required, in sorting through the symbolism and adapting it to yourself, your own particular character, personality and circumstances in life.

Opening the lodge in the first degree

We said, at the beginning, that we would explore the ceremony of opening the lodge after our exploration of the ceremony of initiation. It is not important that you should take part in an opening ceremony before reading what follows. We hope that the following description of the ceremony can shed light on what goes on, either before your own involvement or after it.

You will remember our earlier description of the extent of the lodge, as set out in the lecture:

'. . . in length from east to west, in breadth between north and south, in depth from the surface of the earth to the centre, and even as high as the heavens.'

But note that the physical lodge is twice as long as it is wide, and therefore forms a double cube. Let us think about this as an allusion to a human being. The double cube is said to denote man's dual nature, physical and spiritual, or Divine. The spiritual or Divine side of his nature is an ethereal, non-physical counterpart to his physical body, governed by the same laws and inseparable from it. This duality embodies the principle which says 'as above, so below', just as Jacob's ladder and the hexalpha were links between celestial and terrestrial domains. In this sense, Man is himself the archetype of a lodge, and in the same way that a physical lodge is a co-ordination of different individuals, each one with his own characteristics, so each individual is a composite of the various properties which form his make-up. Just as a physical lodge is characterised by the interaction of its various members, so the individual is characterised by the way his own faculties interact, and by his state of spiritual awareness. The act of opening the lodge is an act intended to alert the mind, shut out material distractions, focus the attention, arouse the officers to their functions and responsibilities, and by all these means to raise the consciousness of all the Brethren present to a higher level.

In the section dealing with the three principal officers of the lodge, we said that, just as God the creator called the world out of nothing, so the Master calls the lodge into being whenever he opens it. In this way, the lodge as a spiritual entity does not exist until it is opened. When the Master knocks, and his knocks are answered by the two Wardens, it is a call to the Brethren that they should turn their attention away from the outer, material world, to focus their energy on their own inner temple, symbolised by the physical lodge. His first words are to call on the Brethren to assist him in opening the lodge, and so we can see that, although it is the Master who has the power to bring the lodge into being, he cannot accomplish this without the mutuality which underlines Freemasonry.

It is to the Junior Warden that he directs the command to see that the lodge is properly tyled, since it is the self, represented by the Junior Warden, which must start the process of closing off the distractions of the outside world. The Master's next command is to the Senior Warden, the soul, to ensure that all present are Freemasons, that they have all made some progress towards light. Now the Brethren may open their hearts in an environment that has been proved to be safe, and the aim here is to assist all those present to expand their consciousness.

There next follows a series of dialogues between the Master on the one hand, and the two Wardens on the other, establishing how many officers there are, their titles and their activities, roles, responsibilities and duties, and the way in which they interact with each other. The Master establishes that there are three principal officers, the Master and the Senior and Junior Wardens, that there are three assistant officers besides the Tyler or Outer Guard, namely the Senior and Junior Deacons and the Inner Guard. Now you would have thought that, given the number of times the lodge has been opened in the past, all this information would be superfluous — surely the Brethren are already well acquainted with all this information? Yet the repetition of this is the very means by which we establish the lodge as an entity, and raise our consciousness as described earlier. Only by being reminded each time of the interaction between the officers of the lodge will they be in harmony and able to work fully with each other.

Since the lodge is a model of the universe (in the macro sense) and of man (in the micro sense), and therefore a model of the 'as above, so below' principle we talked about earlier, we can identify the officers with parts of the lodge, and therefore parts of the psyche, that living part of the man which is beyond the physical, the material.

The Tyler, or Outer Guard, represents the physical world, the outer-sense nature of man, and is stationed outside the door to guard the perimeter between the outside world and the inner temple. The Inner Guard represents the ego, the inner-sense nature, who is stationed inside the temple, by the entrance, and he is the connection between the temple and the outside world. The Deacons are messengers, the conduit through which communications in the lodge flow. The Junior Deacon, stationed near the Senior Warden, is the messenger between the two Wardens, represents feeling and intuition, and can therefore be regarded as one step ahead of the Inner Guard, the ego. The Senior Deacon, stationed near the Master, is the officer who carries instructions and communications from the Master to the Senior Warden, and represents awakening, a stage not yet reached by his junior partner.[18]

We have already spoken of the three principal officers of the lodge, but their roles and functions bear repeating. The Junior Warden represents the self, and is stationed at the mid-point of the temple on the south side, thus marking the sun at its meridian. The Senior Warden represents man's soul, and is stationed in the west, directly opposite the Master. He marks the setting sun; his duty is to close the lodge at the end of the day's work, and to see that the proper wages are paid to the workmen. The Master, being in the east, marks the rising sun, and represents man's spirit, his contact with Divinity. He, or his deputy, is the only one who can open the lodge and confer degrees on aspirants. He it is, also, who should say the prayers at the opening of the lodge, to entreat the Almighty to bless the work of the Brethren in the temple. A lodge cannot be properly opened without seeking Divine aid.

After the prayer, the Master declares the lodge open with the knocks of the degree. This is also the signal for four important things to happen, without which the lodge cannot be truly said to be at labour. First, the Junior Deacon displays the tracing board. Secondly the Immediate Past Master opens the Volume of the Sacred Law and arranges the square and compasses on it, thus constituting the three great lights. He also displays the working tools on, or near to, the Master's pedestal. Lastly, the Senior Warden takes the column lying on his pedestal and places it upright, as an outward sign that the lodge is at labour, and the Junior Warden takes his upright column and lays it horizontal to mark the fact that the lodge is no longer at rest.

Closing the lodge in the first degree

In one sense, the closing of the lodge is the reverse of the opening, except that now it is not necessary to establish the positions and activities of the various officers, except that of the Senior Warden, since he it is who will perform the act of closing the lodge. At the opening, the level of consciousness was raised, and those who are mentally aware of what is going on at the opening, know that there is a heightened state of energy in the temple. So, in the closing, we seek to close and seal the sensitivity of those present, to close that door which we opened by the act of opening the lodge. We seek gently to abate that energy, to let the minds of the Brethren present return to their everyday level of consciousness, and prepare themselves to leave that holy place they have inhabited since the opening.

The Master, assisted by the Junior Warden and the Inner Guard, first satisfies himself that the lodge is still close tyled, that the work in the temple will have been accomplished with integrity and without outside influences. He then, with the assistance of the Senior Warden, calls on the Brethren to stand to order, to remind them of their special status within the walls of the temple. The Master next calls on the Senior Warden to remind the Brethren of the latter's place and responsibilities in the lodge, so that the Senior Warden may then carry out his function of closing the lodge. The knocks of the three principal officers, Inner Guard and Tyler, now mark that the lodge is closed. The Wardens reverse the positions of the columns at the opening, the Junior Deacon covers the tracing board and the Immediate Past Master removes the square, compasses and working tools. He then closes the Volume of the Sacred Law and reminds the Brethren of the need for fidelity.

And you, my new-made Brother, since this process may make new-made Brethren of us all, will by now, we hope, have discovered, have remembered, something of your own nature; will have remembered something like a long-forgotten song learned in childhood, and in that remembering will come to know and to own that song, and to begin to understand and to know your Self. It is a journey full of riches. May all those riches, in time, be yours.

Avenues for exploration in the first degree

The following are some suggestions for avenues to explore. They are only suggestions. There is no 'correct' answer, and this is not meant to be a pursuit of academic excellence! Some of your own ideas will doubtless occur to you, and you should follow them up. The first such 'avenue' has a suggested explanation, to give you a start.

e.g. A comparison of the hexalpha and Jacob's ladder

'The hexalpha has the appearance of a six-pointed star, and is formed of two interlaced triangles. One points to heaven, the other points to earth. Jacob's ladder similarly connects heaven and earth, and the angels of God ascend and descend, linking the two realms. As the two triangles of the hexalpha are inextricable, they indicate the one-ness of God and man and, like Jacob's ladder, form a conduit between the celestial and terrestrial realms.'

Application of the Rule of Three to the working tools

Freedom as having surrendered to others

Freedom from various objects and influences

Need for, and nature of, maturity

Supremacy of God, or supremacy of Man?

Application of the Rule of Three to body, soul, Divine Spirit . . .

. . . and their relationship to wisdom, strength and beauty

Secrets — to be concealed, or to be contained?

The nature of innocence and friendship

The ashlars as two of the principles in a Rule-of-Three triad

Allegory of the dimensions of the lodge

Function of the tesselated border

Relationship between the different lodge officers

Arrangement of the first six officers in the lodge to form a hexalpha

Positions of Wardens' columns at opening and closing

The Self: from unenlightened to enlightened, in the context of the Junior Warden

Different aspects of measuring — measured work, measured actions

Application of the Rule of Three to the ornaments of the lodge

Application of the Rule of Three to the three grand principles of Freemasonry

Glossary of terms used in the first degree

Allegory	a subject with an underlying meaning as well as the literal one
Altar	a raised structure with a plane top, on which to make offerings to a deity; a name sometimes given to the Master's pedestal
Apprentice	*see* Entered Apprentice
Apron	an article of dress worn in front of the body, originally to protect from dirt or injury; the principal clothing of a Freemason, and emblem of innocence and of friendship
Ashlar	a square hewn stone used in building. In Freemasonry there are two forms: the first is roughly cuboid, rough and unhewn, and the second squared and polished
Aspirant	one who, with steady purpose, seeks advancement, privilege or advantage; a person applying to be initiated into Freemasonry, or to be advanced to a higher degree
Badge	*see* Apron
Beauty	a quality which affords keen pleasure to the senses, or which charms the moral or intellectual faculties; the allegorical name of the third of the three pillars supporting a Freemason's lodge, represented by the pillar of the Corinthian order near to the Junior Warden's pedestal
Bible	the Christian holy book, containing also the Old Testament, part of the Jewish holy book (see Volume of the Sacred Law)
Blazing Star	the symbol traditionally present in the centre of the lodge and on the tracing board, representing God; sometimes also called the Glory
Blessing	declaration of Divine favour; benediction
Book of Constitutions	the fundamental rules for the government

43

	and guidance of the Craft
Border	*see* Tesselated border
Brethren	plural of Brother
Brother	a fellow-member of a guild, corporation or order; the term applied by Freemasons to one another
Brotherhood	*see* Fraternity
Brotherly love	an injunction to love our Brethren in Freemasonry; the first of the three Grand Principles (*q.v.*)
Candidate	*see* Aspirant
Canopy (celestial)	the covering of the lodge, and emblematically depicted by seven stars
Cardinal virtues	Temperance, Fortitude (also called Courage), Prudence and Justice
Ceremonial	relating to ceremonies or rites; ritual
Ceremony	an outward rite or observance, held sacred. In Craft Freemasonry there are three ceremonies, one for each degree
Charge	the lecture delivered by the Master to the newly initiated Brother immediately after his initiation, indicating his responsibilities and duties to God, his Fellow men, himself, society, the State and Freemasonry
Chisel	a cutting tool of iron or steel, with the cutting face transverse to the axis, used for cutting wood, metal, stone, bone, etc., and worked by pressure or by the blows of a mallet or hammer; the third of the three working tools in the first degree
Circle	a plane figure bounded by a single line, called the circumference, which is everywhere equidistant from a point within it called the centre
Column	a cylindrical or slightly tapering body of considerably greater length than diameter, erected vertically as a support for some part of a building; in Freemasonry, a small (ca.

44

	60 cm high) pillar, surmounted by a globe, one on the Senior Warden's pedestal, and the other on that of the Junior Warden
Common gavel	a stonemason's setting maul; the second of the three working tools in the first degree
Compasses	an instrument for taking measurements and describing circles, used in Freemasonry in an allegorical sense; the third of the three great lights
Consciousness	knowledge as to which one has the testimony within oneself
Constitutions	*see* Book of Constitutions
Corinthian order	the lightest and most ornamental of the orders of architecture; in the lodge, present on the pillar of beauty near the Junior Warden, the third of the three pillars supporting a Freemason's lodge
Corner stone	the first stone in the foundation of a building, customarily laid at the north-east corner
Courage	*see* Fortitude
Covering (of the lodge)	*see* Canopy
Craft	the practice of speculative Freemasonry
Deacon	name given to the fourth and fifth officers of the lodge. They are messengers; the Senior Deacon communicates between the Master and the Senior Warden, the Junior Deacon between the two Wardens. The Junior Deacon, placed at the right of the Senior Warden in the west, may be regarded as representative of feeling and intuition, and the Senior Deacon, placed at the right of the Master in the east, as representative of awakening. These two officers are responsible for conducting the aspirant during degree ceremonies
Degree	a grade marking attainment or progress in Freemasonry, of which there are three in

	Craft Freemasonry
Deity	*see* Great Architect
Divinity	deity, godhead; the character or quality of the Deity
Doric order	the oldest and simplest order of Greek architecture; in the lodge, present on the pillar of strength near the Senior Warden, the second of the three pillars supporting a Freemason's lodge
Double cube	also called the oblong square, it is twice as long as it is wide, is said to represent the plan of King Solomon's Temple, and is thus the form adopted for a Freemason's temple
Emblem	a concrete visible picture, sign or object representing a principle
Entered Apprentice	a learner of a craft; a Freemason in the first degree
Fidelity	the quality of being faithful
First degree	the first of three grades or levels of attainment in Freemasonry, also called the apprentice's degree
Fortitude	the second of the four cardinal virtues, also called courage, teaching spirit and resolution to counter danger
Foundation stone	*see* Corner stone
Fraternity	a body or order of men organised for religious or devout purposes
Free will	spontaneous will, unconstrained choice to do or act
Freemason	one who, after initiation, practises the art or science of speculative Freemasonry, that is the building of moral and intellectual edifices, to assist in the pursuit of self-knowledge and self-perfection in a fraternal framework
Freemasonry	the fraternity or practice of Freemasons
Furniture	*see* Great Lights
Glory	*see* Blazing Star

God	a superhuman being who is worshipped as having power over nature and the fortunes of mankind
Grace	the Divine influence which operates in men to regenerate and sanctify, and to impart strength to endure trial and resist temptation
Grand Lodge	the governing body of Freemasonry, having jurisdiction over lodges in its territory
Grand Principles	brotherly love, relief and truth, the principles on which Freemasonry is founded
Great Architect	the name given by Freemasons to the Supreme Being; God. The full expression is the Great Architect of the Universe
Great Lights	the Volume of the Sacred Law, the compasses and square. In a Freemasons' temple, the great lights are placed on the pedestal of the Master
Hexalpha	a six-pointed star formed by inverting one triangle on top of another, with the sides interlaced, representing the oneness of God and Man
Hiram Abiff	the principal architect of King Solomon's Temple, responsible for its adornment and beautification
Hiram, King of Tyre	according to biblical legend, he was responsible for supporting King Solomon in the building of the Temple at Jerusalem with men and materials
Honour	title to high respect or esteem; elevation of character; a fine sense of and strict allegiance to what is due or right
Immediate Past Master	that Brother who last occupied the Master's chair before the present Master of the lodge
Initiate	a person admitted with proper introductory rites or forms into knowledge or participation of some principles or observances; a newly made Freemason

Initiation	the act of making a Freemason, by the first degree ritual of Freemasonry
Inner Guard	the most junior of the working officers in the lodge, who guards the door from the inside, and communicates with the Tyler and with the Junior Warden. He may be regarded as representing the inner-sense nature of man (see also Tyler)
Innocence	freedom from moral wrong in general
Inspiration	a special immediate action or influence of the Spirit of God or of some supernatural being upon the human mind or soul
Ionic order	one of the three Greek orders of architecture; in the lodge, present on the pillar of wisdom near the Master; the first of the three pillars supporting a Freemason's lodge
Jacob's ladder	in the legend in the book of Genesis in the bible, Jacob dreamed he saw a ladder connecting heaven and earth, with angels ascending and descending on it
Jewels	an article of value used for adornment; the movable jewels of the lodge are the square, level and plumb rule; the immovable jewels are the tracing board, the rough ashlar and the perfect ashlar
Junior Deacon	*see* Deacon
Junior Warden	*see* Warden
Justice	a personal condition of justice is reached when fortitude, prudence and temperance each plays its part with informed reason in control
Knowledge	state of being aware or informed; consciousness
Landmarks	conspicuous objects in the landscape which serve as a guide; the leading principles of Freemasonry from which there can be no deviation. These include the modes of recognition, the division into three degrees

	of a symbolical character, the government of a lodge by a Master and two Wardens, belief in a Supreme Being by Freemasons, the Volume of the Sacred Law to be an indispensable part of the lodge furniture
Lectures	a system of catechetical lectures by which Freemasons are instructed in the art of Freemasonry
Legend	an unauthentic story handed down by tradition
Lesser Lights	the lights in a lodge placed east, south and west, meant to remind Brethren of the sun (south), moon (west) and Master (east). They are represented by the Ionic column (Master), Doric (Senior Warden) and Corinthian (Junior Warden). These are also referred to as the three great pillars supporting a Freemason's lodge
Level	an implement used in building to determine levels, used in Freemasonry as a symbol of equality. It is the movable jewel marking the rank of the Senior Warden
Lewis	a device made of dovetailed metallic components, also called a cramp, by which stones may be lifted
Liberal arts and sciences	the seven liberal arts and sciences employed by Freemasons are grammar, rhetoric, logic, arithmetic, geometry, music and astronomy
Lodge	an assembly of Freemasons duly warranted by a Grand Lodge
Lodge room	*see* Temple
Mason	*see* Freemason
Masonry	*see* Freemasonry
Master	the first of the principal officers of the lodge. The Master is to rule and direct his lodge. He represents King Solomon and also the contact with Divinity and the Divine Spirit

Materialism	the doctrine that nothing exists except matter and its movements and modifications
Moral	of or pertaining to the distinction between right and wrong, or good and evil, in relation to actions, volitions or character
Mosaic pavement	*see* Square pavement
Mystery/mysteries	a hidden or secret thing; something beyond human reason
Obligation	*see* Vow
Officers	those Brethren charged with the functioning of the lodge. The three principal officers are the Master and the two Wardens, and the four assistant officers are the two Deacons, the Inner Guard and the Tyler. There are in addition, administrative officers, such as the Secretary, Treasurer, Almoner, Charity Steward and Organist
Ornaments of the lodge	in the first degree in Freemasonry, the mosaic pavement, the blazing star and the tesselated border
Past Master	a Brother who has served the office of Master
Pavement	*see* Square pavement
Pedestal	in each lodge, there are three pedestals, one in front of the Master and one each in front of the Wardens
Perambulation	*see* pilgrimage
Perfect ashlar	*see* Ashlar
Piety	habitual reverence and obedience to God
Pilgrimage	a journey to a sacred place as an act of religious devotion. In Freemasonry, the circuit made by the aspirant accompanied by the Deacon, accomplished by passing up the north side of the lodge, across in front of the Master in the east, down the south side past the Junior Warden, and across in front of the Senior Warden in the west, finishing in front

of the Inner Guard. In the first degree there are two pilgrimages: the first proves the aspirant as prepared, inwardly and outwardly to be initiated, and the second, taking place after initiation, proves him as an Apprentice Freemason to the Wardens

Pillar	a detached vertical structure of stone, brick, wood, metal, etc., slender in proportion to its height, used either as a support for some superstructure, or standing alone as a monument etc.; the lodge is said to be supported by three great pillars. These are represented in the lodge by the three lesser lights (*q.v.*) consisting of pillars of the Ionic, Doric and Corinthian orders
Proposer	the Brother who proposes an aspirant as a candidate for Freemasonry
Prudence	a personal condition of prudence is reached when knowledge of how to live (wisdom) informs the reason
Regeneration	the process or fact of being born again spiritually; re-creation or re-formation
Relief	ease or alleviation given through the the removal or lessening of some cause of distress or anxiety; the second of the three Grand Principles (*q.v.*)
Religion	bond between man and God (*Latin:* religare; to bind back)
Ritual	a prescribed order of performing devotional service
Rough ashlar	*see* Ashlar
Rule of Three	the rule that states that, of many groups of three principles, one is active, one passive, and the third acts to maintain a balance between the first two
Sacred Law	*see* Volume of the Sacred Law
Seconder	the Brother who supports the proposition of the proposer

Self	that which in a person is really and instrinsically she or he; the mind or soul
Senior Deacon	*see* Deacon
Senior Warden	*see* Warden
Solomon	King of Israel in the 10th century B.C.
Soul	the spiritual part of man in contrast to the purely physical
Spirit	the animating or vital principle in man; that which gives life to the physical organism, regarded as originating from God
Square	a building implement for proving an angle of 90 degrees; a four-sided equilateral geometric figure; applied in Freemasonry *inter alia* to test moral conduct
Square pavement	the black and white chequered flooring of the lodge
Strength	power in general, whether physical, mental, or due to the possession of resources; capacity for moral effort or endurance; firmness of mind, character, will, purpose; the allegorical name of the second of the three pillars supporting a Freemason's lodge, represented by the pillar of the Doric order near to the Senior Warden's pedestal
Symbol	something that stands for, represents or denotes something else, especially a material object taken to represent something immaterial or abstract
Tassels	the four tassels at the corners of the tracing board (*q.v.*), referring to the four cardinal virtues (*q.v.*)
Tau cross	a cross of three limbs, i.e. in the shape of a T. It is a symbol of salvation and of consecration, also a symbol of trampling evil underfoot
Temperance	the practice or habit of restraining oneself in provocation, passion, desire, etc.; rational self-restraint

Temple	the building or room in which a masonic lodge works and carries on its business
Tesselated border	the design of the edge of the mosaic pavement, also the design round the edge of the tracing board
Tracing Board	normally a wooden board on which are painted or depicted the emblems and symbols of each of the degrees in Freemasonry
Transition	a passing or passage from one condition or action to another
Truth	that which is consistent with fact or reality; faithful; loyal; in Freemasonry, the third of the three Grand Principles (q.v.)
Twenty-four inch gauge	the first of the three working tools in the first degree
Tyler	the last of the assistant officers of the lodge. His place is outside the door of the lodge. He may be regarded as representing the outer-sense nature of man. One of his duties is to prepare aspirants for the ceremony (see also Inner Guard)
Virtue	conformity of life and conduct with the principles of morality; voluntary observance of the recognised moral laws or standards of right conduct
Volume of the Sacred Law	that book which serves as the first of the three great lights in Freemasonry. Often it is the Judaeo-Christian bible, but it can be the holy book of any recognised world religion
Vow	a solemn affirmation; an oath of fidelity sworn by a Freemason at his initiation, with his hand on the Volume of the Sacred Law (q.v.)
Warden	name given to the second and third officers of the lodge. Together with the Master, they are considered the three principal officers. The Senior Warden may be considered

	representative of the soul of man, the Junior Warden representative of the mind and body. In English lodges, the Senior Warden is placed in the west, directly opposite the Master, and the Junior Warden is placed in the south, equidistant from the Master and the Senior Warden.
Wisdom	an understanding of the highest principles of things, that functions as a guide for living a truly exemplary life; the allegorical name of the first of the three pillars supporting a Freemason's lodge, represented by the pillar of the Ionic order near to the Master's pedestal
Working tools	in the first degree, the twenty-four-inch gauge, the common gavel and the chisel, the symbolism of which is used in a speculative sense
Worshipful Master	*see* Master

---

[1] Dyer, *Symbolism in Craft Freemasonry*, page 128
[2] *The Lectures of the Three Degrees in Craft Masonry*, page 32
[3] MacNulty, *The Way of the Craftsman*, page 57
[4] Wilmshurst, *The Meaning of Masonry*, page 36
[5] MacNulty, *The Way of the Craftsman*, page 58
[6] ibid. page 61
[7] Dyer, *Symbolism in Craft Freemasonry*, page 131
[8] *The Lectures of the Three Degrees in Craft Masonry*, page 78
[9] ibid. page 53
[10] Haunch, *Tracing Boards — Their Development and their Designers*, page 1
[11] Wilmshurst, *The Meaning of Masonry*, page 94
[12] MacNulty, *The Way of the Craftsman*, page 72
[13] Browne, *Master Key*, page 29
[14] *The Lectures of the Three Degrees in Craft Masonry*, page 69
[15] Haunch, *Tracing Boards — their Development and their Designers*, page 5
[16] MacNulty, *The Way of the Craftsman*
[17] *The Lectures of the Three Degrees in Craft Masonry*, page 75
[18] MacNulty, *The Way of the Craftsman*, page 42

The Second Degree

'The youth, who daily farther from the east
must travel, still is Nature's priest,
and by the vision splendid
is on his way attended;
at length the man perceives it die away,
and fade into the light of common day.'
William Wordsworth

Up to now, we have had many instances which portrayed Freemasonry as a journey. More than that, Freemasonry is a series of journeys within journeys. We saw how, in the first degree, within the integral journeying from west to east, from darkness to light, from un-knowing to knowing, there were yet more pilgrimages, more journeys within those journeys. Now that you have passed the degree of a Fellow Craft, you can see that the second degree, like the first, was a composite journey, and both degrees part of the whole masonic journey.

The previous degree dealt with birth, in many of its aspects: birth of the man, but also birth of knowledge, knowledge of the self. In this second degree, we deal with life after birth, the journey through life, and the development of the self with its new-found knowledge and increasing wisdom. But you will also learn (or you have already learned) that this degree bears certain echoes of the former degree, echoes but not exact counterparts, as for example the approach of the aspirant to the Master's pedestal.

The object of this degree is something we touched on in the former — the smoothing of the rough ashlar to make of it a perfect ashlar. Bear this in mind as we journey now through a landscape which is at once strange, yet familiar; a landscape which we have to discover, to remember.

A test and some retrospection

Let us start with the questions you answered before being admitted to a Fellow Craft's lodge. In reality, these questions are a vestige, a left-over of a much more elaborate lecture system, much of which is very rewarding to study.[19] Yet even in that which survives, there is much valuable insight:

'Q.   Where were you first prepared to be made a Mason?
A.   In my heart.'

Here, of course, is the central point of your admission, and it bears repeating — we think with our mind, but we intuit with our heart. So, Freemasonry is not an academic pursuit, nor one requiring scholarship. Freemasonry requires that we use intuitive faculties and our feelings, in nurturing knowledge and in gaining wisdom.

Next, you were reminded of the importance of preparation for the first degree ceremony, and the account of the physical preparation reminded you of the inner preparation it was necessary to undertake. The questioning now entered into the place and time of your initiation:

'Q.   Where were you made a Mason?
A.   In the body of a lodge, just, perfect and regular.
Q.   And when?
A.   When the sun was at its meridian.'

The lodge was the only place where you could be made a Mason, in the body of all the Brethren assembled, to make you one with them. The fact that you were made a Mason at the allegorical time of midday was important — you will remember that it is the Junior Warden in the south who represents the sun at its meridian, and that in the nature of man he stands for the mind/body, the self. In this sense, he is the emblem of the new aspirant. And lastly, you were reminded of trials and approbations, of testings, of the means of making progress:

'Q.   How do you know yourself to be a Mason?
A.   By the regularity of my initiation, repeated trials and approbations, and a willingness at all times to undergo an examination when properly called on.'

Although you were yet to be prepared by the Tyler, the nature of the questions and of your answers were such as to alert you, to prepare you for this onward journey, the journey of life.

But you still needed a further forewarning in order later to enter a Fellow Craft's lodge. Once you had answered the questions leading to the second degree, the Master entrusted you with a password. Let us consider this for a moment. When you were admitted to the temple in the first degree, you were not given a password, and indeed there was none you could be given. Instead, you were admitted, being 'free and of good report'. But you had not yet learned how to be in harmony and consonance with what was taking place in the temple. That harmony and consonance came with the restoration of light, harmony between you and the other Brethren, but also harmony with what was taking place. Here, before your advancement, the Master was about to open the lodge in the second degree before re-admitting you. Here, where there was no hoodwink, you would be able to take a full part in the proceedings of a Fellow Craft's lodge, and it would therefore be necessary for you to be in harmony with that second degree raised level of consciousness. This is the reason why the password was communicated to you before you left the temple to be prepared. You had to be ready to be a part of the new, expanded consciousness of this new degree.

There is another perspective: you left the first degree lodge, and the lodge was then raised in your absence to the second degree, to a higher level of consciousness. How was that achieved? Think back for a moment to your experience in the first degree lodge. There was an energy present, such as is generated by a body of people all concentrating on a particular subject. The very same phenomenon is in evidence when the lodge is opened in the second degree, and the result is a higher state of consciousness.

Before we move on, there is one further important aspect. You were told that the password is represented in a Fellow Craft's lodge by an ear of corn near to a fall of water, signifying plenty, a potent symbol of fruitfulness and sustenance. As an emblem, we could regard the aspirant as representing the ear of corn, the sign of forthcoming fruitfulness, relying on the water to sustain it. Here is a hint that life's journey will not be accomplished without nourishment, both material and spiritual.

Preparation

Probably the most important outer feature distinguishing this new degree from the first, was that you were not now in darkness — you could see all that was going on around you. And since you now know that initiation, in the sense we have spoken of it, makes of you an individual ashlar, free from the bedrock in the quarry, it follows that that new freedom calls on an individual responsibility for your own actions and reactions. The absence of the hoodwink was a mark of your advancement. Your freedom has assured you of the right to exercise that responsibility; you are now an individual, and can choose whether to exercise it or not.

Your preparation outside the door of the temple proceeded in much the same way as in the previous degree. Yet there were important differences. Not only was there no hoodwink, there was no cable tow either. Such an emblem of submission was no longer necessary. Your own sense of responsibility makes *imposed* submission unnecessary, and in its place we have your own *voluntary* obedience. You will recall the mention of this in the charge after initiation:

'Your obedience must be proved by a strict observance of our laws and regulations, by prompt attention to all signs and summonses, by modest and correct demeanour in the lodge, by abstaining from every topic of political or religious discussion . . . and by perfect submission to the Master and his Wardens . . .'

The remaining aspects of your preparation were that your left arm, left breast and right knee were made bare and your left heel was slipshod, almost the opposite of the preparation in the first degree. As you will see, when we look at the detail, many of the aspects of the second degree form a mirror image of the first; hence many symbols, such as the baring of the left arm and right knee are the correlation of, or complementary to, the first degree, the two halves symbolically making a whole.[20]

Access to privileges

Before you were admitted to the temple, there was a similar series of questions and answers at the door as in the first degree, but this time the emphasis was on the progress you had made, recommending you to be considered for advancement. Remember that in the first degree there was no password; you were to be given access to the privileges

'. . . by the help of God, being free and of good report.'

And how, in contrast, did you hope to obtain the privileges of the second degree?

'By the help of God, the assistance of the square, and the benefit of a password.'

This is important; as you would expect, the name of God was invoked in both cases, but now your freedom and your reputation were not in question. In their place, you were required to be in possession of the password in order to be at one with the proceedings in a Fellow Craft's lodge, and your progress towards this new level of consciousness and of knowledge was to be assisted by one of the most important symbols in Freemasonry — the square.

The Square

You will remember this emblem, probably in the first instance in the steps you took in advancing to the pedestal in the first degree, where your feet were placed in the form of a square, or as the second of the three great lights, the other two being the Volume of the Sacred Law and the compasses. The square also made its appearance as the first of the three movable jewels of the lodge, and as such it formed the jewel on the collar of the Master. If you think about the square, the angle of ninety degrees, you will begin to realise how universal a symbol it is, and we hope to show you its growing importance in Freemasonry. Think for a moment how frequently we have already met with it, apart from the three instances we have just mentioned. To state perhaps the obvious, it is the right-angle at the corners of most of the objects we have discussed. The rectangle of the tracing board and of the apron are both bounded by four squares. The temple, the double cube, is bounded by twenty-four of them. Two of the movable jewels, the level and plumb rule, when put together, form the two arms of the square, which is itself the first movable jewel. We put our feet in the form of a square to form the tau cross, and again when placed at the north east part of the lodge. In most lodges, the movements of the officers and the pilgrimages of the aspirant are accomplished by 'squaring' when changing direction. The square is all around us; it is everywhere. A masonic researcher once said that 'The square, in the sense both of the tool and of the shape, is the basic element — the atom — of the masonic structure'.

We saw in the first degree how the square is that emblem which regulates our lives and actions, and its symbolism reminds us of the duties we owe to ourselves, to develop our moral character. We saw also that the true and proper signs by which to know a mason were 'all squares, levels and perpendiculars'. Although the square as a symbol of morality and correct behaviour pervades all of our masonic activities, it is nowhere more important than in this, the second degree. It is a symbol which at once calls us to attention, defines what we do, and is a yardstick, or a magnetic compass, to prove that we are on the right path. If we have dealt with the square here at some length, it is because its importance as a symbol cannot be overstated.

Admission

Now you were once again admitted to the temple, and once again the Master called on you to kneel for the benefit of prayer. In the first degree, we spoke of lodges as regular, well-formed, constituted lodges. This regularity, formation and constitution applies equally to the degree ceremonies. One aspect of this is that no regular masonic labour is ever countenanced which has not first invoked God's blessing and His grace. Once again, nothing was to be undertaken without first invoking the grace of God. This time the Master, on your behalf, sought the continuance of God's aid, and prayed that

'. . . the work begun in Thy name be continued to Thy glory and evermore established in us by obedience to Thy precepts.'

Thus although you were embarked apparently on a new journey, it was in truth a continuation of the journey, the work, already begun in the first degree, and was securely confirmed as work following the ordinances of God Himself.

Two pilgrimages

After the prayer, you set off on a journey now familiar to you, this time accompanied by the Senior Deacon. Remember that in the section devoted to the opening of the lodge in the first degree, we identified the Deacons as messengers, the conduit through which communications in the lodge flow. The Junior Deacon is the messenger between the two Wardens, and represents feeling and intuition. The Senior Deacon is the officer who carries instructions and communications from the Master to the Senior Warden, and represents awakening, a stage not yet reached by his junior partner. This stage therefore, the second degree, will represent for you that awakening which allows you to employ the feelings and intuitions of which you became aware in the first degree.

As you were not now hoodwinked, you could appreciate that your journey round the lodge was in a clockwise fashion, starting in the west, progressing through the lodge on the north side to the east, and thence by the south side back to the west. You may have already realised that you were following the course of the sun. From its setting in the west until its rising next morning in the east, all is dark. In the northern hemisphere, at night the sun passes behind the earth on the west side to re-appear in the east. We mentioned this in the first degree, when we spoke of the significance of being placed at the north east corner, the place where you emerge from darkness into light. This is another reason why the lesser lights are placed east, south and west, in a configuration which, significantly, leaves out the north side.

This pilgrimage was one on which you would prove yourself to the Junior Warden as a Freemason. You may ask why this was necessary, since the Master would hardly have agreed to this new ceremony if your credentials had not been established. But remember one of the questions you had answered before leaving the temple to be prepared:

'Q. How do you know yourself to be a mason?
A. By the regularity of my initiation, repeated trials and approbations, and a willingness at all times to undergo an examination when properly called on.'

'Repeated trials and approbations.' Here, as elsewhere, the repeated stating of your condition and of your intentions is an indispensable part of your progress.

Your new journey-within-a-journey was a continuation of trials and approbations. This was not some organisation where you could be awarded a university degree on payment of a fee. This was no quick-fix advancement, and the repetition of questions was in itself a certain level of instruction for you, as well as for the Brethren present in the temple. As with the repetition in the lodge opening and closing, it set up the level of energy and awareness of all those present, and it did so in a spiritual way.

Your second pilgrimage was to prove to the Master and Brethren that you were properly prepared and in possession of the password. Once again, here is a confirmation of the status quo, where the process of advancement incurred the repetition of all the elements at each stage. You proved yourself once again, this time with your new-found parole.

Advancement

The Senior Warden, representing as always the soul, satisfied that you were properly proved, announced to the Master, representing the Divine Spirit, that you had been properly prepared to be passed to the second degree. The Master directed that you should be 'instructed to advance to the *east* in due form'. In the first degree, at the corresponding point in the ceremony, the Master directed that you should 'advance to the *pedestal* by the proper steps'. There was of course no way that you could know, in your earlier state of darkness, that the Master's pedestal was in the east. Stop and think how much you have learned since that time. You were aware now that to advance you must approach the east. You were aware that:

'As the sun rises in the east to open and enliven the day, so the Master is placed in the east, to open the lodge, and employ and instruct the Brethren in Freemasonry . . .'

and, further, it is in the east that the three great lights are situated. In your enlightened state, materially as well as spiritually, you were well able to grasp the significance of the east as the source of light, knowledge and wisdom.

Now you were to approach the east in a very different manner. Before, you approached by three unequal steps, each one in the form of a square, but all three on the same level. These steps, you will remember, increased in length as you increased in confidence in your new-found profession. But in the second degree, you approached the east as if ascending five steps of a winding staircase. You were ascending, to a higher floor, a higher level, where greater truths than those in the previous degree might become clear to you. You were still approaching the three great lights, of which the greatest was the Volume of the Sacred Law, and to do so, by your five steps, you had completed a circuit of a quarter-circle. It is of course no accident that the fourth part of a circle is still the 90 degrees of the square, the emblem of correct morality, and the emblem you are meeting more frequently as your journey progresses.

A further vow

You now stood symbolically at the door of the middle chamber of the temple, and we will have more to say about this when we explore the tracing board of this degree. But before the three great lights, and before the Master, your access to the Divine Spirit, the Master required of you that you should make another solemn vow, kneeling, with your left arm supported in the angle of the square. There was no need to ask you to swear all the points of your first vow. This new, shorter vow was essentially in two parts; first that you would not reveal aspects of this second degree to Entered Apprentices, and secondly that you would act as a true and faithful Craftsman. Truth and fidelity — two important virtues with which to arm yourself, not only to ensure correct behaviour towards other Fellow Crafts in this degree, but also virtues necessary to gain admission to the middle chamber of the temple. Truth, you will remember, is the third of the three grand principles on which Freemasonry is founded, and perhaps the most important of the three. It is linked to uprightness, honesty and purity in life as in actions. Fidelity is one of the hallmarks of this degree, and we will speak about it again in relation to the entrusting of the secrets.

As in the first degree, the Master now called your attention to the position of the square and compasses, which, as you know, was subtly different from their position in the previous degree, half revealing a part of the compasses. Remember the words of the Master at this point:

'. . . *you are now in the midway of Freemasonry, superior to an Entered Apprentice, but inferior to that to which I trust you will hereafter attain.*'

The key word here is 'midway'. The Master was marking your progress along the path, away from your first experience in the first degree, and indicating a new experience which would ultimately lead to something even greater. And as you later saw, the top of the winding staircase placed you at the door of the middle chamber of the temple.

Entrusting and instruction

You now took the second regular step in Freemasonry, a step identical to that in the first degree, in which your feet came naturally into the form of a tau, or T-shaped cross, the emblem of generation or creation. Yet, although identical in *form*, this step was different in *intent*, since to take it placed you in the position to receive the sign, token and word of this new degree. As you remember, these are in reality not secrets, but rather modes of recognition, each one with its own symbolism, not revealed to the outside world, as to do so would devalue them and dissipate their energy and the energy that you will need on your journey.

The signs taught you that by outward forms you could impress on your own heart the importance of fidelity and perseverance. If you think about the threefold sign, you will remember that it forms four squares, once again stressing the importance of that symbol. The first part of the sign may remind you of faithfulness. Fidelity is often applied as faithfulness to a cause or faithfulness to others. Consider for a moment other synonyms for fidelity. These include allegiance, constancy, dependability, integrity, loyalty, trustworthiness. Now, while all of these may be applied to our dealings with others, many of them, if not all, can also be applied to our own building. Trustworthiness implies being true; true to our own nature and our own instincts. This leads to integrity, the wholeness, completeness and soundness of our moral bedrock, and is closely allied to the uprightness of the third movable jewel, the plumb rule.

The second part of the sign guides us towards the virtues of constancy and resolution. Perseverance is a quality we have already met, as the way to avoid the double jeopardy in the first degree; you will remember that we must neither hold back nor rush forward — either course endangers us. The way forward, literally as well as figuratively, is by steady perseverance, steady onward progress, above all not allowing ourselves to be defeated by contrary influences. Here, in the second degree, the virtue of perseverance is applied to the progress we make in transforming our rough ashlar into a perfect ashlar.

Think back for a moment to some of the symbolism of the first degree at the corresponding point in the ceremony. You will remember that the Master instructed you in the symbolism of one of the pillars at the entrance to King Solomon's Temple. As you were now in possession of the distinctive qualities of the second degree, he instructed you in the symbolism of the other pillar, its partner. These two pillars form an important part of what happens in Freemasonry from now on, and their symbolism is almost as broad and comprehensive as that of the square itself. We will have more to say about them when we consider the second degree tracing board.

Journeying towards a new mark

With these distinctive second degree qualities now communicated to you, you advanced on a new perambulation or pilgrimage, accompanied still by the Senior Deacon, to prove yourself in the new degree, yet in a form well known to you. Once again, the repetition served to confirm the status you had now acquired in your own mind, and in the minds of those around you. And once again, at the end of this journey, the Senior Warden presented you to the Master as the aspirant

'. . . on his being passed to the second degree, for some further mark of your favour . . .'

and as you might expect, the Master directed that you should from now on wear a new badge, distinguishing or marking your progress as a Fellow Craft. The Master added

'. . . the badge with which you have now been invested points out that, as a Craftsman, you are expected to make the liberal arts and sciences your future study, that you may the better be enabled to discharge your duties as a mason, and estimate the wonderful works of the Almighty.'

Further study

The Master specifies here a course of study, a study which would not just broaden your mind, but would enable you to be a better man, a more enlightened Freemason, and would broaden your appreciation of the creation and harmony of the world. Study, and education, are often misunderstood and misused. Plutarch, writing at the beginning of the first millennium, said

'A student mind is a fire to be lit, not a vessel to be filled.'

This is not study intended to fill your mind with data. This was study meant to inspire you — to set you alight with a desire for progress, to set you alight with ideas and insight into the true nature of your journey. The tools which the science of Freemasonry proposes are the seven liberal arts and sciences. These are grammar, rhetoric, logic, arithmetic, geometry, music and astronomy. By grammar, we learn the proper use of words, to enable us clearly to understand the writings of those more enlightened than we are, to stimulate the learning of which our journey is composed. By rhetoric, we may acquire skill in expression, enabling us to persuade by the strength of our argument, and ultimately to teach. A study of logic will enable us to guide our reason while directing our enquiries after truth. Arithmetic, the science of numbers, will enable us to calculate, as will geometry, which further enables an appreciation of form and the relationship between structures, in every sense. Music enables an appreciation, in a real, tangible way, of harmony and of its opposite, discord, and also of rhythm. These last three concern the harmony, proportion and wholeness of the created world. Astronomy, a complex science, seeks to enable our appreciation of the infinite works of the Creator.

See how often we have used here the word 'enable', since all of this is constructed with you in mind — the enabling of your own faculties, leading you to knowledge of, and perfection of, your Self. Once again, think of the words of part of the prayer in the first degree:

'. . . assisted by the secrets of our masonic art, he may the better be enabled to unfold the beauties of true godliness . . .'

There lies the secret of learning. Like everything else in Freemasonry, learning is a journey, a journey on which we experience life and 'unfold' the truths from within our own Self.

Following the sun

You were now placed at the south-east part of the lodge. In the first degree, you were placed at the north-east part, so in your new situation, you had moved round the temple in a clockwise fashion, moving with the sun, from the east, to the south-east. In this situation, the Master addressed you again on the need for study:

'. . . as in the previous degree you made yourself acquainted with the principles of moral truth and virtue, you are now permitted to extend your researches into the hidden mysteries of nature and science.'

So, while the apprentice work in the first degree was concerned with subduing the sense-nature and its impulses, the next stage is the stimulation and development of the intellect of the heart. The investigation of the hidden mysteries of nature, namely your own nature, and science, the science of knowing, will lead you 'to the throne of God Himself', revealing the ultimate potential of your own being. But notice that, whereas earlier we used the word 'enable', now the Master says that you are *'permitted'* to extend your researches. That permission has come about in virtue of this new degree: you would not have been permitted to undertake this course of study as an Apprentice Freemason, since you were, at that stage, still working on the pursuit of moral truth and virtue, and had not reached the stage where you could follow such study.

New working tools

Think back for a moment to the movable jewels of the lodge which you learned about in the first degree — they were the square, which is the badge of office of the Master, the level, that of the Senior Warden, and the plumb rule, marking the Junior Warden. So these are the symbols illuminating those officers of the lodge who represent, respectively, the Divine Spirit, the soul, and the mind/body, or the self. Here in the second degree, those same symbols were made accessible for you, as working tools, in two senses. In the material sense:

'. . . the square is to try, and adjust, rectangular corners of buildings, and assist in bringing rude matter into due form; the level, to lay levels and prove horizontals; the plumb rule, to try, and adjust, uprights, while fixing them on their proper bases.'

As before, although they appeared in the form of mechanical instruments, so too they were there to supply insight on our journey. In the allegorical sense:

'. . . the square teaches morality, the level equality and the plumb rule justness and uprightness of life and actions.'

There is an important difference between the working tools in the first degree, and those in this new degree. The implements of the first degree, the twenty-four inch gauge, the common gavel and chisel, were tools of action, in hewing and cutting stone in the one sense, and in forming our moral character in the other sense. In this new degree, the tools are tools of testing. In the section dealing with the first degree, we learned that the square is the implement with which we test the perfect ashlar, to ensure that it has been properly worked by the experienced mason. So also are the other two working tools in this degree tools of testing, to see that the work has been properly carried out. Testing the perfect ashlar is one of the principal activities in the second degree, since the square 'teaches us to regulate our lives and actions'. Remember that earlier, in talking about the square, we said that it is the symbol which at once calls us to attention, defines what we do, and is a yardstick, or a magnetic compass, to prove that we are on the right path. The level, you will remember, is the symbol denoting equality, demonstrating that when we are born, we are all equal and that, when we die, our only distinctions will be those of goodness and virtue. The plumb rule is a reminder of Jacob's ladder, in that it too connects heaven and earth. As an upright emblem, it speaks to us of rectitude and of truth. The Master's address to you concluded with the words

'Thus by square conduct, level steps and upright intentions, we hope to ascend to those immortal mansions, whence all goodness emanates.'

'Ascend to those immortal mansions'. Think back for a moment to what we said in the first degree. At the door of the temple, you had reached a turning point. Your entrance marked the beginning of your initiation into Freemasonry, the end of your spirit's descent into matter, and its subsequent return to God. In the second degree, you ascended the winding staircase. The whole symbolism and imagery in this degree is one of ascending, and the three working tools, from the passage above, are there to assist us in that ascent.

70

Two pillars

After you had left the temple to restore yourself, you were re-admitted, and at this point the Master delivered the tracing board lecture. It was here that much of the symbolism, particularly that of the winding staircase, was expanded upon.

Here the architecture, form and symbolic function of King Solomon's Temple come to the fore. We use that temple as an allegory, first as an allegory of the temple of humanity, and then as an allegory of our own personal spiritual edifice. Remember that the rough ashlar was removed from the bedrock and became an individual stone. We are now employed in perfecting that stone. Every Freemason eventually dedicates himself as a perfect ashlar in the construction of the temple, into whose fabric he will be incorporated.

The first feature of King Solomon's Temple to which the Master called your attention was the two great pillars at the porchway of the east entrance. Now you knew the names and the significations of those two pillars and, more importantly, their meaning once they were conjoined. So you could now trace your progress from the first faltering steps of your initiation, in darkness and in a state of un-knowing, to your present situation, which denoted that stability comes from strength of the spirit. Your whole journey was of course not yet complete, but you could begin to see something of the nature of your progress.

In the eighteenth century, the layout of the temple in English Freemasonry was significantly different to the present day. The Master, as now, was placed in the east but, as we mentioned in the first degree, the two Wardens were placed in the west, one either side of the door, and of course each one had the column of his office nearby, usually in the form of a large pillar. We said, in the first degree, that the Wardens' function was as a kind of gatekeeper, deriving from the Roman god Janus, the god of gates and doors, beginnings and endings. He was represented by a double-faced head, one face looking in, the other out. Janus represents the transition between primitive life and civilization, and the growing to maturity of a young person, and that symbolism is clearly relevant to your present state of advancement in Freemasonry.

Although the door to the masonic temple was in the west, the opposite of the entrance to King Solomon's Temple in the east, the aspirant still had to enter the temple, in any degree, between the Wardens. Let us for a moment, in our imagination, put those columns back at the west end of the lodge, side by side. We once again have the pillar on the left, and its partner, with a different signification, on the right, and the conjoining of the two being of most importance to us in this degree. Traditionally, the right-hand side was considered superior to the left in matters of strength, and so indeed does our right-hand pillar represent the Fellow Craft who, through his progress, is made a stronger, more stable part of the structure.

Wages

In the lecture, the Master talked about the masons who were employed in the building of King Solomon's Temple. These, he told you, consisted of Apprentices and Fellows, in other words first and second degree masons.

'The Entered Apprentices received a weekly allowance of corn, wine and oil; the Fellow Crafts were paid their wages in specie, which they went to receive in the middle chamber of the temple.'

The Apprentices, having travelled only a short way along the path, have not yet achieved much spiritual growth. Their needs are basic — corn, wine and oil will provide them with sufficient bodily sustenance, and these three substances represent the most basic human nourishment. The Fellows on the other hand could only receive their wages, which were in specie, that is money, in the middle chamber of the temple, so these wages, these rewards, were spiritual rewards. The middle chamber is an allegory of the heart, where the Divine spark resides, as we saw in the previous degree. In all mystical tradition, this heart is spoken of as the place where dwells God in man. It is in reality a state of mystical experience, where the soul sees, and for a brief moment becomes one with, the Divine Source of all. As the aspirant progresses towards the middle chamber, this becomes more apparent.

A winding staircase

'After our ancient Brethren had entered the porch, they arrived at the foot of the winding staircase which led to the middle chamber.'

But they were not free to ascend this staircase, since the Junior Warden, representing, as we know, the body and mind, would not let them pass until they had given him tokens of their entitlement to ascend. These tokens are emblematic of our right to advance, and are gained only after suitable spiritual progress. These, you will remember, were the tokens not of one degree or the next, but tokens leading from the first to the second degree, so they represent a transition. The password is depicted by an ear of corn near to a fall of water, two elements figurative of fruitfulness. In one tradition, the ear of corn is likened to the Fellow Craft himself, whose nourishment and growth are symbolised by the fall of water.

Is it not interesting to see here the essential differences in tone between the first and second degrees? In the first degree, we were surrounded by actual danger, and symbols of it. Difficulties were put in our path to test us. Darkness surrounded us, but we sensed that we were proceeding, steadily, towards the light, and we sensed that, if we were steady and purposeful, we would overcome. In this degree, we have met only mild approbations — our figurative and spiritual environment has been one filled with life, light and a journey through a land of fruitfulness where, if we work, we may receive wages, or rewards, of more than material worth. The differences are striking, and are meant to be so.

To ascend therefore we have to prove ourselves. Afterwards, we ascend the winding staircase, consisting of three, five, seven or more steps. Let us pause here for a moment and look at one of the second degree lectures. In relation to the number of steps, it has this to tell us:

'Q.   *Why three?*
A.   *Rule a lodge.*
Q.   *Why five?*
A.   *Hold a lodge.*
Q.   *Why seven or more?*
A.   *Make it perfect.*

Q. Who are the three that rule a lodge?
A. The Master and his two Wardens.
Q. Who are the five that hold a lodge?
A. The Master, two Wardens and two Fellow Crafts.
Q. Who are the seven that make it perfect?
A. Two Entered Apprentices added to the former five.
Q. Why do three rule a lodge?
A. Because there were but three Grand Masters who bore sway at the building of the first Temple at Jerusalem, namely Solomon King of Israel, Hiram King of Tyre, and Hiram Abiff.
Q. Why do five hold a lodge?
A. In allusion to the five noble orders of architecture, namely the Tuscan, Doric, Ionic, Corinthian and Composite.'[21]

Three rule a lodge. This was one of the triads we met with in the first degree — the Junior Warden, representing the mind/body, the Senior Warden representing the soul, the Master, emblematic of our access to the Divine Spirit. Reduced to the bare elements, the first degree needed no more than those three officers for our initiation. But now we have a group of five to consider, the five who hold a lodge being two Fellow Crafts added to the rulers. We have here a sense that, among those who have charge of the lodge, the addition of two Fellow Crafts will be necessary for the added work in the second degree. And since you are now a Fellow Craft, and you have received your wages in specie, you too are entitled, even expected, to play your part in having charge of the lodge, and thereby to grow in spirit.

The middle chamber

Arrived at the door, your access to the middle chamber of the temple was controlled by the Senior Warden, representing as always the soul, who, like his junior partner at the bottom of the staircase, would not let you pass until you had given him tokens of your entitlement to proceed. These are now not tokens of transition from one degree to the next, but the real sign, token and word of this new degree, emblematic of the progress you have made. Without proof that you had made this advancement, access to the middle chamber, and the wages or rewards you would there receive, would be impossible. Let us once again remind ourselves: we do not follow the path of a quick-fix solution. We have to work to gain the spiritual remuneration we have come here to seek. Now you have been admitted to the middle chamber, and you have a foretaste of what may await you in the holy of holies, face to face with God, for here you are acquainted with His name. You sense that your progress, through moral truth and virtue, through the intellectual pursuits of your own heart, through the paths of heavenly science, has led you to the throne of God, and the promise of being united with Divinity. For a moment, be still, and ponder all this, and all that it imparts.

Tools and materials

Now that your progress has led you to the completion of the second degree, it is important to remember the main aspects of the working tools. You will remember that, while the working tools in the first degree were characterised as tools of action, here the square, level and plumb rule are spoken of as tools of testing, and proving, that the work is well-executed — a sort of quality control.

'The square is to try, and adjust, rectangular corners of buildings and assist in bringing rude matter into due form; the level to lay levels and prove horizontals; the plumb rule to try, and adjust, uprights while fixing them on their proper bases.'

So in its operative sense, the square proves, verifies and authenticates square corners, to ascertain their *truth*. The level does the same for the horizontal elements of the building, as does the plumb rule for vertical elements. In the allegorical sense, likewise, these tools verify and authenticate the *truth* of morality:

'The square teaches us to regulate our lives and actions according to the masonic line and rule, and to harmonise our conduct in this life, so as to render us acceptable to that Divine Being from whom all goodness springs, and to whom we must give an account of all our actions.'

75

Remember, in Freemasonry the square is all around us. It is the ever-present model, of life as of actions.

In its allegorical sense, the level also has insights into truth:

'The level demonstrates that we are all sprung from the same stock, partakers of the same nature, and sharers in the same hope. . . no eminence of situation ought to make us forget that we are Brothers; for he who is placed on the lowest spoke of fortune's wheel is equally entitled to our regard, as a time will come — and the wisest of us knows not how soon — when all distinctions, save those of goodness and virtue, shall cease, and death, the grand leveller of all human greatness, reduce us to the same state.'

The plumb rule, the third of this important triad, is the third of these working tools but also, you will remember, that movable jewel adorning the Junior Warden, and situated therefore in the south, the position of the midday sun. Its insights are no less important, and touch, symbolically, on the very nature of truth:

'The infallible plumb rule which, like Jacob's ladder, connects heaven and earth, is the criterion of rectitude and truth. It teaches us to walk justly and uprightly before God and man, neither turning to the right nor left from the paths of virtue . . . neither bending towards avarice, injustice, malice, revenge, nor the envy and contempt of mankind, but giving up every selfish propensity which might injure others. To steer the bark of this life over the seas of passion, without quitting the helm of rectitude, is the highest perfection to which human nature may attain. And as the builder raises his column by the level and perpendicular, so ought every mason to conduct himself towards this world; to observe a due medium between avarice and profusion; to hold the scales of justice with equal poise; to make his passions and prejudices coincide with the just line of his conduct, and in all his pursuits to have eternity in view.'

In the first degree, we spoke of the rough ashlar as representing the aspirant before any spiritual progress has been made. This is the object on which the working tools of the first degree are brought to bear. The lecture has an insight here. The rough ashlar, as we know, is a stone, rough and unhewn as taken from the quarry, until:

'. . . *by the industry and ingenuity of the workman, it is modelled, wrought into due form, and rendered fit for the intended structure. This represents man in his infant or primitive state, rough and unpolished as that stone until ... he is rendered a fit member of civilised society.*'

The object in the second degree is to work on that stone. When perfected, that stone will be:

'. . . *a stone of a true die or square, fit only to be tried by the square and compasses . . .*'

namely a stone representing the enlightened man, whose life:

'. . . *can no otherwise be tried and approved than by the square of God's word, and the compass of his own self-convincing conscience.*'[22]

Opening the lodge in the second degree

When we dealt earlier with your preparation for the second degree ceremony, the ceremony of passing, we spoke of the importance of the password giving you access to the second degree lodge. We said that there was a need for you to be in harmony and consonance with this new, raised-consciousness lodge, so it is right to infer that the opening in this degree raises the consciousness of the Brethren. They actually and symbolically pass from the first degree state, the knowledge of moral truth and virtue, to the higher state, implying an intellect guided, not by the brain, but by the heart.

The physical form of the temple is of course unaltered. We assume that the lodge is already open in the first degree. When the Master now knocks, he is answered as before by the Wardens. It is a call to the Brethren to direct themselves towards this higher, intellectual plane. Their energy is about to be focused, but now to a higher degree than previously. Again, this opening will be achieved in a spirit of mutual understanding, by all the Brethren present.

The Master calls in turn on the two Wardens, first to see that the distractions of everything not pertaining to the degree are shut out, then to prove all present as Freemasons. Remember, this is not so much to ensure that there are no unentitled persons present, but rather to call the Brethren to attention. The next question by the Master is to the Junior Warden, to confirm that he is a Fellow Craft Freemason, and to ascertain by what instrument he will be proved as such. It will come as no surprise to you that the instrument by which he wishes to be proved is the square, that ever-present emblem. Pause here for a moment, and think about the layout of the temple. Imagine a circle, with its centre at the mid-point of the temple floor, the arc of which touches the Master in the east, the Senior Warden in the west, and the Junior Warden in the south. If two lines are drawn from the ends of the diameter (the Master and the Senior Warden) to meet at a third point on the circumference, say the Junior Warden, the rules of geometry tell us that they will form an angle of ninety degrees. So it is that the Junior Warden stands, physically, in the angle of the square, the instrument by which he will be proved.[23]

Now the Brethren prove themselves Craftsmen, in other words they raise their energy level to the second degree, and with this, the lodge is correctly formed. The Master calls on all present to:

'. . . supplicate the Grand Geometrician of the Universe that the rays of heaven may shed their influence to enlighten us in the paths of virtue and science . . .'

and hence to allow us to engage in the pursuit of knowledge, that crucial aspect of the second degree.

As soon as the Master declares the Fellow Craft lodge open, three important things happen to confirm the new raised status. The Junior Deacon replaces the first degree tracing board with that of the second degree, the Immediate Past Master rearranges the square and compasses on the Volume of the Sacred Law, and then replaces the working tools of the first degree with those of the second. The lodge is now ready for second degree labour.

Closing the lodge in the second degree

The aim of closing, as it was in the first degree, is to close and seal the sensitivity of those present, to close the open door of the Fellow Craft's lodge, and to gently abate the raised energy of this degree. The Master, as before, satisfies himself that the lodge is still close tyled. The words he uses are *'prove* the lodge close tyled'. The Brethren then stand to order again, to remind themselves of their special status within the walls of the temple.

What happens next is of crucial significance to Fellow Craft Freemasons. While the Brethren are still standing in the sign, the Master has the following exchange with the two Wardens:

'*Master:*   *Brother Junior Warden, in this position what have you discovered?*
Junior Warden: *A sacred symbol.*
Master: *Brother Senior Warden, where is it situated?*
Senior Warden: *In the centre of the building.*
Master: *To whom does it allude?*
Junior Warden: *The Grand Geometrician of the Universe.*'

This sacred symbol, alluding to God himself, is situated in the centre of the building, that point from which we earlier drew the circle touching on the three principal officers. That is its physical location. Its allegorical location however may be in one of two places: the centre of the building of the temple of humanity, which we seek to build, or the centre of the building of our own temple, placing the Deity at our own centre which, as you know, is that point within a circle round which you cannot err. Our journey to the middle chamber, the centre of that building also, resulted in us receiving our wages.

We could regard these spiritual wages as being of two kinds. Payment may be made in two directions: payment for work well done, but also repayment of debts owed. We may have repayments to make for past sins or misdemeanours, committed against individuals or against humanity in general. This is a drawing up of the balance sheet, a payment of old scores, and an opportunity for us to make restitution for past offences. Then, when we are satisfied that we have purged ouselves in this way, we may receive our spiritual reward, and we are fit to be in the middle chamber, to increase our awareness of and proximity to God, since this is the route that leads you 'through the paths of heavenly science, even to the throne of God Himself'. Hence, in the closing prayer, the Master reminds us that:

'. . . wherever we are, and whatever we do, He is with us, and His all-seeing eye observes us, and whilst we continue to act in conformity with the principles of the Craft, let us not fail to discharge our duty to him with fervency and zeal.'

The Senior Warden then closes the lodge, the Junior Deacon replaces the first degree tracing board, and the Immediate Past Master adjusts the position of the square and compasses and replaces the first degree working tools. So it is that the heightened energy level of the lodge is gradually brought down to that of a first degree lodge.

And so ends your second journeying. This stage was the middle stage, a journey from outside the temple proper to a special place, the middle chamber. In this degree you were to discover something which, unknowingly, you had sought — the manifestation of God, the purging of old wrongs, and the payment of spiritual wages. It is of course still the mid way of Freemasonry, and there is, as you know, progress to come. But this degree has a special significance of its own, a degree of tranquillity, yet with a sense of achievement, a sense of responsibility earned. You progressed by ascending, since moral and spiritual progress is an upward progression. If this had been a concrete journey, rather than a figurative one, you might at this stage be asked to stop, rest awhile, and take stock of all that has passed. So too on this allegorical journey you should pause and reflect, since you have achieved much, but much has to be assimilated before you proceed to the third stage. Think, ponder, go back over what you have read here, and see if some of the stones are beginning to fall into place. The building is progressing. And you, at once the builder and the building, can feel some sense of achievement at having made progress.

Avenues for exploration in the second degree

As in the section on the first degree, these are only suggestions, and you are encouraged to develop some avenues of your own.

The nature of the 'body of the lodge'

An ear of corn near to a fall of water

Obedience vis-à-vis responsibility

Universality of the square both as geometric shape and as instrument for proving

Change in the arrangement of the square and compasses on the Volume of the Sacred Law in the second degree

A Freemason as a part of the temple of humanity; a Freemason as his own edifice

Deacons as messengers or conduits for information

Wages, actual and symbolic

Different modes of approaching the east

To ascend the winding staircase one turns through 90 degrees, one quarter of a circle

Different aspects of proving — the lodge, the person

Truth, uprightness, integrity, and the symbols of these

Aspects of fidelity and perseverance

Allegory of pillars, separate and joined

Nature and Science

Action and testing/proving

Middle Chamber as allegory of the heart

Comparison of the working tools in the first and second degrees

Application of the rule of three to the second degree working tools

Two parallel lines on the first tracing board; two pillars on the second tracing board

Glossary of terms used in the second degree

This glossary should be used in conjunction with that at the end of the first degree section of this book.

Apron	an article of dress worn in front of the body, originally to protect from dirt or injury; the principal clothing of a Freemason, and emblem of innocence and of friendship; in the second degree, in altered form from that of the first degree
Ashlar	a square hewn stone used in building. The rough ashlar is appropriated to the first degree; the perfect, or squared and polished stone, is appropriated to the second degree.
Aspirant	one who, with steady purpose, seeks advancement, privilege or advantage; a person applying to be initiated into Freemasonry, or to be advanced to a higher degree
Badge	*see* Apron
Candidate	*see* Aspirant
Ceremonial	relating to ceremonies or rites; ritual
Ceremony	an outward rite or observance, held sacred. In Craft Freemasonry there are three ceremonies, one for each degree
Compasses	an instrument for taking measurements and describing circles, used in Freemasonry in an allegorical sense; the third of the three great lights
Composite order	*see* Five noble orders of architecture
Corinthian order	*see* Five noble orders of architecture
Craft	the practice of speculative Freemasonry
Craftsman	*see* Fellow Craft Freemason
Deacon	name given to the fourth and fifth officers of the lodge. They are

messengers; the Senior Deacon communicates between the Master and the Senior Warden, the Junior Deacon between the two Wardens. The Junior Deacon, placed at the right of the Senior Warden in the west, may be regarded as representative of feeling and intuition, and the Senior Deacon, placed at the right of the Master in the east, as representative of awakening. These two officers are responsible for conducting the aspirant during degree ceremonies

Doric order   *see* five noble orders of architecture

Ear of corn near to a fall of water
    the symbol relating to the password leading from first to the second degree

Fellow Craft   *see* Fellow Craft Freemason

Fellow Craft Freemason   the name given to one who has passed to the second degree in Freemasonry

Fidelity   the quality of being faithful

Five noble orders of architecture
    the architectural orders denoted by the names Tuscan, Doric, Ionic, Corinthian and Composite, studied in an allegorical sense. The study of these, together with that of the seven liberal arts and sciences, is the chief labour of the second degree

Grand Geometrician   the name given by Freemasons in the second degree to the Supreme Being; God. The full expression is the Grand Geometrician of the Universe

Intellect   perception, discernment, meaning, sense, understanding; that faculty of the mind and heart by which one knows

Ionic order   *see* five noble orders of architecture

Junior Deacon   *see* Deacon

Junior Warden   *see* Warden

84

Knowledge	state of being aware or informed; consciousness
Lesser Lights	the lights in a lodge placed east, south and west, meant to remind Brethren of the sun (south), moon (west) and Master (east). They are represented by the Ionic column (Master), Doric (Senior Warden) and Corinthian (Junior Warden). These are also referred to as the three great pillars supporting a Freemason's lodge
Level	the second of the second degree working tools, also the second of the movable jewels. It is an emblem of equality
Liberal arts and sciences	the seven liberal arts and sciences employed by Freemasons are grammar, rhetoric, logic, arithmetic, geometry, music and astronomy
Lodge	an assembly of Freemasons duly warranted by a Grand Lodge
Middle Chamber	King Solomon's Temple was surrounded by a sub-structure three storeys high, of which the middle storey was called the Middle Chamber
Password	a word given to permit an aspirant to proceed to a degree higher than the one for which he is currently qualified
Perambulation	*see* Pilgrimage
Perfect Ashlar	*see* Ashlar
Perseverance	constant persistence in an undertaking or steadfast pursuit of an aim. In theological terms, continuance in a state of grace, leading finally to a state of glory
Pilgrimage	a journey to a sacred place as an act of religious devotion. In Freemasonry, the circuit made by the aspirant accompanied by the Deacon,

accomplished by passing up the north side of the lodge, across in front of the Master in the east, down the south side past the Junior Warden, and across in front of the Senior Warden in the west, finishing in front of the Inner Guard. In the second degree there are three pilgrimages: the first proves the aspirant in the first degree, the second proves him as prepared, inwardly and outwardly, to be raised to the second degree, and the third, taking place after he has been passed, proves him as a Fellow Craft to the Wardens

Pillar a detached vertical structure of stone, brick, wood, metal, etc., slender in proportion to its height, used either as a support for some superstructure, or standing alone as a monument etc.; the lodge is said to be supported by three great pillars. These are represented in the lodge by the three lesser lights (*q.v.*) consisting of pillars of the Ionic, Doric and Corinthian orders. In the second degree the two pillars at the porchway or entrance of King Solomon's Temple are dealt with. The left-hand pillar has a first degree significance, and the right-hand pillar in conjunction with its partner has a second degree significance

Ritual a prescribed order of performing devotional service

Rough Ashlar *see* Ashlar

Second degree the second of three grades or levels of attainment in Freemasonry, also called the Craftsman's or Fellow Craft's degree

Senior Deacon *see* Deacon

Senior Warden *see* Warden

Seven liberal arts and sciences

see Liberal arts and sciences

Square — a building implement for proving an angle of 90 degrees; a four-sided equilateral geometric figure; applied in Freemasonry *inter alia* to test moral conduct

Symbol — something that stands for, represents or denotes something else, especially a material object taken to represent something immaterial or abstract

Tracing Board — normally a wooden board on which are painted or depicted the emblems and symbols of each of the degrees in Freemasonry. A separate design is used in each degree, particular to that degree

Transition — a passing or passage from one condition or action to another

Tuscan order — *see* five noble orders of architecture

Vow — a solemn affirmation; an oath of fidelity sworn by a Freemason at his initiation, and subsequently also on his advancement to each of the other two degrees. It is sworn with his hand on the Volume of the Sacred Law

Warden — name given to the second and third officers of the lodge. Together with the Master, they are considered the three principal officers. The Senior Warden may be considered representative of the soul of man, the Junior Warden representative of the mind and body. In English lodges, the Senior Warden is placed in the west, directly opposite the Master, and the Junior Warden is placed in the south, equidistant from the Master and the Senior Warden.

Winding staircase — traditionally the staircase leading from

| | the north porch of the entrance of King Solomon's Temple at ground level, to the Middle Chamber of the Temple, at first-floor level |
| Working tools | in the second degree, the square, level and plumb rule, the same implements as the movable jewels of the lodge. Their symbolism is used in a speculative sense |

---

[19] *The Lectures of the Three Degrees in Craft Masonry*
[20] Dyer, *Symbolism in Craft Freemasonry*, page 132
[21] *The Lectures of the Three Degrees in Craft Masonry*
[22] ibid.
[23] Dyer, *Symbolism in Craft Freemasonry*, page 133

The Third Degree

'Truth is within ourselves; it takes no rise
from outward things, whate'er you may believe.
There is an inmost centre in us all,
where truth abides in fullness; and around,
wall upon wall, the gross flesh hems it in,
this perfect, clear perception — which is truth.
A baffling and perverting carnal mesh
binds it, and makes all error: and to know,
rather consists in opening out a way
whence the imprisoned splendour may escape,
than in effecting entry for a light
supposed to be without.'
Robert Browning

The runner rounds the corner and squares up for the home straight. 'Last lap!' the bystanders cry, as he puts everything that he's got into a final burst of energy. This is the culmination of everything he has thrown into the race, and he's determined that the result will be a record achievement.

A runner in this situation may have many thoughts in his head. He may be looking forward to the end of the race, knowing that he can then relax. He may have it in mind to break a record. He is certainly looking forward to a sense of having achieved something, by any standards.

An aspirant for the third degree in Freemasonry is in a similar situation, but importantly different. He will certainly want to give it his best. To him, 'last lap' will however not mean that he is looking forward to relaxing. He will certainly be putting a lot into it, knowing that it is the culmination of the formal masonic journey. If all has gone well, he will indeed have a sense of having achieved something remarkable.

But by now you will have many impressions of this great, sublime experience. Once again, let us take things slowly and examine this third journey in its constituent parts. You will for instance have noticed that, whereas the second degree was in many respects an extension of the first, this third degree, by contrast, had many more features that set it apart completely from the other two.

As the first two degrees dealt with birth and life, so this degree dealt with one of the great mysteries to which we shall one day be subject: the mystery of death. Here, as you know, we dealt not so much with physical death, but the death of the material side of the self, to be reborn at a higher level of consciousness. This was an echo of the first degree, where we sought to subdue the material senses and physical passions, in order to attain to moral growth, rebirth in a sense now familiar to you. In another sense, we have here a sublime application of the Rule of Three — the first degree as the active principle, the second as the passive, both of them co-ordinated and given form and meaning by the third degree. Your rough ashlar is well on the way to emerging as a perfect ashlar, but this degree was to impart to you something much more profound — the culmination of the knowledge and understanding of your own nature, and your knowledge of, and oneness with, God.

A further test and password

The questions asked of you before leaving the lodge to be prepared, referred to the previous degree, and were again a recapitulation:

'Q. On what were you admitted?
A. The square.
Q. What is a square?
A. An angle of ninety degrees, or the fourth part of a circle.
Q. What are the peculiar objects of research in this degree?
A. The hidden mysteries of nature and science.'

Nature and science. Mysteries which were hidden. You had started on the quest for knowledge of your own nature, as also on the

science of knowing in general, that which the ancient Greeks called *gnosis*, and defined as *a special knowledge of spiritual mysteries*. These were hidden mysteries, and you will remember that they are hidden because it is in the searching, finding, unveiling and decoding that their value lies. You had progressed to the middle chamber of the temple, namely your own heart, there to be paid your wages, namely wages of a spiritual worth. The two great pillars, combined, signified the stability you had attained on your journey, a stability you would now have need of in the extreme trials of the third degree.

Now for a further entrusting. You will remember that you here needed, as in the second degree, the benefit of a new password to place you on that further, higher plane, the third degree lodge that you were shortly to enter. This new password, you were told, was emblematic of worldly possessions and was the name of the first artificer in metals. This, surely, is a paradox? In the first degree, you were deprived of all money and metallic substances, because they represent the attractive power of temporal possessions and earthly belongings. Why then do we need reminding of this, here on the threshold of the third degree? Because to attain the light of self-knowledge promised (and partly conferred) by the first degree, it is essential to be free of such things. It is essential for us to be detached from them so that we are content, if need be, to be divested of them, if they stand in the way of being initiated into something better. How then are we to interpret this new password? The answer is that, by the password communicated to you, you were represented as not yet being entirely free of worldly possessions. It was a warning, a flag raised; a reminder that you needed to be sure you were purged, as far as possible, of their attractions.[24]

Preparation and admission

We spoke a little earlier of the third degree being the co-ordinating principle of the other two, in a Rule-of-Three triad. Here, we have a graphic example of what that means; your physical preparation for the third degree was a combination of the preparation in the other two degrees, a conclusion of them.

Now think back, and compare the questioning at the door of the temple in the second and third degrees. You were said, in the second degree, to hope for the privileges of that degree

'. . . *by the help of God, the assistance of the square, and the benefit of a password . . .*'

whereas in this, the third degree, your hopes rested on:

'. . . *the help of God, the united aid of the square and compasses, and the benefit of a password . . .*'

In the second degree we spent some time talking about the importance of the first of these, the square. The counterpart here is the *union* of the square and compasses, two of the three great lights, which are now not some far-off emblem on the Volume of the Sacred Law, but are symbolically given into our hands as implements to aid us on this third part of the epic journey. As the great lights however, the position of these two very important symbols changed subtly from one degree to the next, and here, in the third degree, their position shows the completeness of their association, the compasses now being freed from the constraints of the square. Hence the completeness of the emblem of square and compasses is a mark of how sublime this third degree would prove to be.

Now you were admitted to this third degree lodge, with its stark contrast to the second. Almost total darkness. Let us pause here for a moment, and reflect on the question of darkness and light. One reason given in the old lectures for being hoodwinked in the first degree was to prevent you from seeing the form and nature of the temple, and the dress of the lodge members. But as you now know, the symbolism in the temple is not apparent merely by looking at it; this is a symbolism which becomes apparent through study, through work. So the restoration of light to you, as an individual, was emblematic of gaining inner light, an indication of the power of the revelation of symbols. So light here was the light of knowledge, the *gnosis* we referred to. And the material light to which you were restored in the first degree was *general* light, replacing *personal* darkness. Here, by contrast, you were admitted to a Master Mason's lodge, where darkness has descended on all present, save a small

93

light in the east. This then is no personal, individual darkness, but rather a general darkness. The lesson of this darkness will become apparent as the ceremony proceeds.

For anyone entering a dark room from the light, a period of adjustment is necessary, even to see any small amount of light that may be present. Here, the Brethren in the temple had already had the opportunity to adjust before you entered, so that you alone had difficulty discerning the faint light in the east, and the people and objects round it. This too is emblematic of your transition from the second to the third degree, for even the possession of the password would not be enough for you to be at one with what was happening here. At this stage, physically and figuratively, you yet lacked the means of responding to this faint and feeble light. And what that proper response would be, we shall explore later.

A sublime prayer

Once inside the temple, as in the two former instances, the prayer would set the tone for the coming ceremony:

'*Almighty and Eternal God, Architect and Ruler of the universe, at Whose creative fiat all things first were made, we, the frail creatures of Thy providence, humbly implore Thee to pour down on this convocation assembled in Thy Holy Name the continual dew of Thy blessing. Especially we beseech Thee to impart Thy grace to this Thy servant, who offers himself a candidate to partake with us the mysterious secrets of a Master Mason. Endue him with such fortitude that in the hour of trial he fail not, but that, passing safely under Thy protection through the valley of the shadow of death, he may finally rise from the tomb of transgression, to shine as the stars for ever and ever.*'

'Almighty and Eternal God'. This is an intentional reference to the idea that you were about to enter into a concept of eternity as the summation of your journey. To proceed towards this, God's blessing was again invoked, but also grace to you in particular. 'Impart Thy grace to this Thy servant.' The word grace has many meanings. The one intended here is undoubtedly:

'. . . the Divine influence which operates in men to regenerate and sanctify, and to impart strength to endure trial and resist temptation.'

So too God is implored to endue the aspirant with the second of the four cardinal virtues we learned about in the first degree, namely with fortitude, elsewhere called courage, 'that in the hour of trial he fail not', but that through His protection, you might 'rise from the tomb of transgression, to shine as the stars for ever and ever'. Here is embodied a great lesson of this degree. 'Transgression' refers to sin. Since, on your progress in the two former degrees, you have been engaged in moral development, a lack of that increase in morality would leave you still in need of progress away from materialism and towards light, now hinted at as light eternal. Now we can begin to understand the warning given by the password, that our journey, away from material desire and gain, must be single-minded, unfaltering. By that route, the light eternal would eventually be complete in your own completeness, so that you would shine with light eternal, or 'as the stars for ever and ever', elsewhere expressed in the words 'world without end', or 'in saecula saeculorum'. The power of this prayer is compelling, and the words may ring in your head for some time to come.

Three pilgrimages and advancement

In the first degree, you were accompanied by the Junior Deacon on your journey, and in the second, by the Senior Deacon. In this degree, as a sign that you might need more support on this journey, and also as a culmination of the former two, you were accompanied by both Deacons.

Once again, you confirmed the grades of achievement which you had reached. On the first pilgrimage, you proved yourself to the Junior Warden as an Apprentice. Again, you were following the course of the sun, despite the surrounding near-complete darkness. The phrase 'repeated trials and approbations' was again relevant, as it was also on your second pilgrimage, where you were called on to prove yourself as a Craftsman, this time to the Senior Warden. Your third pilgrimage once again established that you were properly prepared and in possession of the password. Again, this was to substantiate not only the stage you had reached, but also that the new-found password would entitle you to proceed.

Advancement can, of course, only take place west to east, since it is in the east that the Master and the three great lights are situated. But here it had a special significance, in that your journey from darkness to light had a real, tangible connotation; namely, you were progressing towards the only light present, the light at the Master's pedestal, dim though it was.

If you had expected advancement towards the three great lights to be as straightforward as in the former degrees, you would have been mistaken. Here was a most unexpected obstacle. In order to approach the light, you had to step over a grave. In order to approach light therefore, you had to traverse the very negation of light and life, namely the ultimate symbol of death. Had you not succeeded in negotiating this perilous path, the light would not have been attainable. The grave over which you stepped was not that grave destined to contain your own dead body, but rather the grave where your own lower self now lies buried, and over which you had to walk before attaining the heights toward which you were now well advanced. Self-sacrifice and self-negation were essential before you could be raised to a higher plane.

You may have noticed that the number of steps in each degree, three in the first, five in the second, and seven in the third, have an allusion to the number of steps said to compose the winding staircase, as also to the number of Freemasons making a perfect lodge:

'Q. After our ancient Brethren had given those convincing proofs to the Junior Warden, what did he say to them?
A. Pass, ...
Q. Where did they then pass?
A. Up the winding staircase.
Q. Consisting of how many steps?
A. Three, five, seven or more.
Q. Why three?
A. Rule a lodge.
Q. Why five?
A. Hold a lodge.

Q.   Why seven or more?
A.   Make it perfect.'[25]

Think also for a moment about the differences marking the steps of advancement in the three degrees. The first degree steps were level. The second degree steps ascended. The steps in the third degree were neither level nor ascending. They necessitated overcoming an obstacle, and this obstacle was emblematic of our evolution from the death of materialistic pursuits, pursuits which we seek to overcome and reject in order, with the last four steps, to draw nearer, unimpeded, to the light, a light at once physical and symbolic.

A third vow

Cast your mind back to the position you were in before making your first degree vow. Your right hand was on the Volume of the Sacred Law. Your left hand held the compasses, one point presented to your heart. In the second degree, your left arm was supported in the angle of the square. In this third degree your left arm was not employed with any of these concrete symbols; instead, both hands were free, for the symbols were now in your heart and had no need of outward signs. Instead, you were free to place both hands on the Volume of the Sacred Law, the better to confirm this sacred, sublime vow, the culmination of everything to which you pledged yourself.

The first part of your new vow concerned secrecy, and you will remember the importance of secrecy in containing, rather than concealing, an aspect common to all three degrees. In the second part, you pledged yourself to adhere to the principles of the square and compasses. It bears repeating that the square is a symbol which at once calls us to attention, defines what we do, and is a yardstick, or a magnetic compass, to prove that we are on the right path. The compasses comprise that instrument with which we describe the circle, four times the angle of ninety degrees. Crucially for us in this third degree, the circle is also the emblem of eternity; it has no beginning and no end, and constantly renews itself. This is not the first time we have met the symbol of the circle. Think back to the first degree tracing board:

'In all regular, well-formed, constituted lodges, there is a point within a circle round which the Brethren cannot err . . .'

so that the circle itself, besides being an emblem of the eternity we spoke of earlier, is of crucial importance in finding our own centre.

The third part of this new vow has a unique importance for Master Masons:

'I further solemnly engage myself to maintain and uphold the five points of fellowship in act as well as in word . . .'

Here the practice of mutuality in a very comprehensive way was brought to the fore, the sublime virtue of brotherly love. Your hand should be a sure pledge of brotherhood, always concerned not to let a Brother down. You should embrace difficulty and danger if the needs of a Brother require that you should do so. You should at all times put his needs before your own. You should unhesitatingly guard anything that he confides in you, and do anything necessary to safeguard his good name and reputation. The well-being of those close to him should be as dear to you as if they were your own relatives and friends.

There is an important parallel here with the deprivation of money in the first degree. In that degree, it was essential for us to be detached from material concerns so that we were content, if need be, to be divested of them if they stood in the way of being initiated into something better. In like manner, in this third degree, we should be content, even ready, to sacrifice comfort and safety if the needs of a Brother require it.

Now you were able, even in the dim light afforded, to appreciate the new arrangement of two of the great lights, the square and compasses, arranged now so that the completeness of the whole might be apparent to you, so that you might be:

'. . . at liberty to work with both those points, in order to render the circle of your masonic duties complete.'

But the position of the three great lights was of greater significance still, for now, as you could see, even by the glimmering ray, for the first time the compasses predominated in their arrangement with the square. Now for the first time the spirit, represented by the compasses, took precedence over material matters, represented by the square. The transformative action of the three great lights was complete.

Retrospection

At this point, you were led backwards until you stood at the foot of the grave. You will have noticed that, in these pages, we have often recapitulated on what has gone before, in order to impress on your mind the connections and continuity of the whole. Here the Master does the same, by confirming much of what has passed in the two former degrees, and by reflecting on them. We spoke about 'repeated trials and approbations', but here the Master speaks of:

'. . . *that last and greatest trial, by which alone you can be admitted to a participation of the secrets of this degree . . .'*

Let us examine this retrospection of the Master. He referred to your state of helplessness at your initiation, an emblem of birth, the entrance on your mortal existence. Your initiation had taught you lessons of equality and mutual dependence, and of mutual support. It taught you the virtues of beneficence and charity and, importantly, it taught you:

'. . . *to seek the solace of your own distress, by extending relief and consolation to your fellow-creatures in the hour of their affliction.'*

This was an echo of the five points of fellowship in your vow. And, the Master reminded you, the whole had the effect of submitting you to God's will, to accept gladly those burdens which adherence to His will might place upon you. In this way, once your heart had become free of sensory influences, contrary influences, once it had become receptive to truth and to wisdom, it was a heart that you might then dedicate to God, and to your fellow-men.

'Proceeding onwards, still guiding your progress by the principles of <u>moral</u> truth, you were led, in the second degree, to contemplate the <u>intellectual</u> faculty . . .'

and by these means to tread the paths of heavenly science, otherwise known as knowledge, or *gnosis*, enabling you to approach the throne of God Himself, referring to your journey to the middle chamber in the second degree. In other words, the development of your own personal morality, though not yet complete, had led you to the point where you were able to appreciate the intellectual dimension of your journey, using the intellect of the heart. This expansion of the heart was such that you had attained a closer acquaintance with God, which allowed you a glimpse that, in the words of the Christian bible, 'the kingdom of God is within you'. This is the meaning of the words:

'. . . the secrets of nature, and the principles of intellectual truth, were then unveiled to your view . . .'

since we speak here of your own nature, and the intellectual truth to which your own heart attains.

Deeper darkness

You were now, however, to be prepared, symbolically and by contemplation, for the closing hour of existence, and to be instructed how to die.

Throughout your journey in the first and second degrees, from the moment the hoodwink was removed, light in one form or another had shone on your work; physical light, certainly, but also other figurative light, the light of the liberal arts and sciences, the light of the prevalent tone of Freemasonry, the light shed on your journey by your Brethren also, and ultimately your own inner light. Now you were practically deprived of all light, except that light within you. A very wise masonic mentor once wrote:

'Hitherto, although guided by that light [within], the aspirant has progressed in virtue of his own natural powers and efforts. Now the

time has come when those props have to be removed, when all reliance on natural abilities, self-will and rational understanding must be surrendered, and the aspirant must abandon himself to the transformative action of his Vital and Immortal Principle alone ... he must surrender all that he has hitherto felt to be his life, in order to find life of an altogether higher order.'[26]

You began, in the first degree, to ascend out of the gross materialism of your former life, on your return to God; you arrived at the middle chamber and learned something more of the nature of the Deity so that now, before proceeding to the ultimate mystery, you were in a position where the death of the old self was imminent, thereby leading you to an appreciation of eternity and what that could mean for you. And on the way, there was another important lesson, one linked again to the five points of fellowship, namely that:

'. . . *death has no terrors equal to the stain of falsehood and dishonour.'*

A legend

Here followed a legend, the core of the symbolism of this sublime degree. Like all legends, we have little way of ascertaining its factual truth. This is its strength, since we are here concerned, as you know, with its philosophical truth, a truth made plain through allegory. As you know, the power of this whole system is allegory, ideas and words presented by images, ideas so powerful that they can only be represented by allusion, by implication, by example. To give you some idea of this, in ancient cultures the name of God could not be pronounced or spoken aloud; so powerful was it, that it could not be given verbal expression.

Allegory is clothed in words, and by now you will have learned that the words in themselves are without meaning until we de-code what they are telling us. Here we have the legend of a man, a principal architect at the building of King Solomon's Temple, a man skilled in artistry. The lecture in the first degree, speaking of the three great pillars supporting a Freemason's lodge, reminds us of their names, wisdom, strength and beauty, known to us as the three lesser lights, and tells us that they further represent Solomon, King of Israel; Hiram, King of Tyre; and Hiram Abiff:

'. . . Solomon, King of Israel, for his wisdom in building, completing and dedicating the Temple at Jerusalem to God's service; Hiram, King of Tyre, for his strength in supporting him with men and materials; and Hiram Abiff, for his curious and masterly workmanship in beautifying and adorning the same.'[27]

So the subject of our legend here is no less than that man said to symbolise the third of the lesser lights, the symbol of beauty, who was prepared to lose his life rather than betray a trust.

Think back to what we said about containing secrets. If we reveal them, if we betray that trust, we endanger ourselves first and foremost. To progress towards a greater spirituality, to benefit from moral and intellectual growth, we have to guard what we know, what has been revealed to us, to make the energy work in our selves. In our modern materialist world, the word betrayal sounds archaic. We can however still render the sense of the word in modern language. A traitor is someone who is disloyal, who fails to honour a promise, who breaks trust, who deceives. We can all think of instances in our daily lives where people we know have been guilty of this, or instances where we have ourselves fallen short of the mark of trust. The ritual speaks of Hiram's 'unshaken fidelity', and that sums up the sentiment of what we aspire to.

But there is a more important dimension here, for us as Freemasons. The figurative death we refer to, as we mentioned already, after all that we have experienced in the first two degrees, is the final death of the old materialist Self, to be reborn, in greater light, on a higher plane. It is death to the concept of one's Self, which most of us spend a great deal of energy constructing, but which in truth is not the most important part of the Self. By this death, we may realise our identity as a spiritual being which possesses a Self, rather than a Self which contains a spiritual being.[28]

Raising

And so you suffered, symbolically, the death of one who is subjected to the triumph of evil over good. This was the lowest point, the point at which the soul must voluntarily submit to absolute abandonment and rejection, without the hope of earthly help, and as you know, the first two attempts to raise you proved useless. The only hope of salvation lay in the intervention of Divine aid, when no less than the hand of Divinity itself reached down from above, and with the grip of almighty power, achieved that which human intervention had failed to do, namely to raise the regenerated man to union with God, in an embrace of reconciliation and of perfect union, the embrace signified by the five points of fellowship.

Piercing the darkness

Once the aspirant has been raised, the Master exhorts him to see the light of a Master Mason as darkness visible. What are we to make of that apparent paradox? It must surely be one of the allegories in Freemasonry that is most rich with meaning. Let us think again about light and darkness.

There is a philosophical puzzle often proposed, which is this: a red book is lying on a table in a lighted room. When the light is switched off, the room is in complete darkness. In the darkness, is the colour of the book still red? We have no way of knowing. We are in a similar situation here. The light of a Master Mason is darkness visible. But we have no physical light switch with which to illumine the space we seek to investigate. What we do have, if we have been successful in following this degree thus far, is the knowledge, the *gnosis*, the Divine inspiration with which to work out what is taking place. By the grace bestowed by God in following the paths of Freemasonry, first those of moral truth and virtue, then those of nature, science and intellect of the heart, and now in this degree a more profound knowledge of our Self, we receive yet more light even than the figurative light bestowed by the first degree. In other words, we possess the talent, skill or power to see this darkness for what it is. The ritual tells us that this darkness visible:

'. . . *serves only to express that gloom which rests on the prospect of futurity* . . .'

103

and we need to understand that 'express' here means to press out, to push aside, to dispel that gloom. We may be reminded of Henry Vaughan, who wrote:

'There is in God — some say —
A deep, but dazzling darkness; as men here
Say it is late and dusky, because they
See not all clear.'

Being able to see clearly where all before was darkness, shows us then that future which awaits us in life, a future that does not end with death, since eternity, as we have seen, is now within our grasp, and we may indeed attain to life everlasting. But it needs work and the help of God to translate this darkness. It is indeed

'. . . that mysterious veil which the eye of human reason cannot penetrate unless assisted by that light which is from above.'

The key phrase here is 'human reason', since, as you now know, relying on our reason, on rationality and on material constructs, will get us only so far; we need the spirit, in this case Divine inspiration, to help us achieve our ultimate goal: profound inner knowledge and perfection.

From darkness to light

And we are given implements to help us. You will remember, at the start of this degree, you were admitted to a Master Mason's lodge, where darkness had descended on all present, save a small light in the east. But, and this is important, it was not *totally* dark. There *was* a light, however small. There was yet hope. This small light was at once an aid and a task; an aid because without it you would have achieved nothing, and a task because the very nature of your work in this degree is one of increasing that light. And by that glimmering ray, you were able to discern the emblems of mortality, emblems with which you could now work to extract inspiration from the allegory, and also emblems steering you towards:

'. . . that most interesting of all human studies, the knowledge of yourself.'

In order to contemplate on your inevitable destiny, you will *need* knowledge of yourself. But also by contemplating on your inevitable destiny, you will *gain* knowledge of yourself. The pursuit of self-knowledge is not something with set parameters. You are exhorted here, in the words of the ritual, to continue to listen to the voice of nature, your own nature, we may call it the song within you, which bears witness that even in your *mortal* frame resides an *immortal* principle, namely your own Being. And this vital and immortal principle is that which gives you the strength, 'a holy confidence', that God will be with you in your further journeying through life.

The chequered pavement, as we saw in the first degree, points out the diversity of objects in the creation. There is no more stark contrast to our senses than black and white, darkness and light, evil and good, chaos and harmony and, ultimately, death and life. This flooring of a Freemason's lodge is in truth an emblem of our passage through our temporal existence. As your life will continue to present you with dangers, setbacks, contrary influences of every kind, so too you will now have the strength, the light, to counter them. Another wise masonic mentor, in relation to the glimmering ray at the Master's pedestal, tells us:

'As the Master was present in the lodge, his light remained, as the spiritual and moral teaching which he gave would still be with a Brother at the time of death, although those grand luminaries, the sun and moon, would no longer be of use to him. By the help of this teaching, he would triumph over death and succeed to life eternal, symbolised not only by the raising itself, but by the restoration of general light to the lodge.'[29]

At this point the Master, who had stood in the south, addressing you in the north, exchanged positions with you, so that you moved, physically, from the north, the place of darkness, to the south, the place of the midday sun, thereby figuratively a place where more light might be available to you. This then is a turning point in more than one sense, for the insights of the heart were about to encompass also further instruction.

Signs and significations

Now you were able to take the third regular step in Freemasonry. You will recall that this step was identical in form to the former two, a step in which your feet came naturally into the form of a tau, the T-shaped cross, the emblem of generation or of creation. It is also a symbol of trampling evil underfoot and vanquishing it. As the ritual expresses it:

'. . . the Lord of Life will enable us to trample the king of terrors beneath our feet, and lift our eyes to that bright morning star, whose rising brings peace and salvation to the faithful and obedient of the human race.'

The lesson here is quite clear: generating our own spiritual splendour, our own bright morning star, is possible if we reject evil and combat it, especially within ourselves.

The signs of a Master Mason proceed from the sign of a Fellow Craft, namely the h.s. or s. of p., combined with the s. of f. The first two signs in this third degree allude to the account of Hiram's death and the discovery of his body. The p. sign, apart from the physical connotations it carries, relates to the centre of our own being. The point within a circle, the centre of the lodge is, as you know, the point from which a Freemason cannot err. A Freemason is a lodge, and the centre point is that point from which he cannot err, here allegorically indicated by the p. sign. You will remember we said in the first degree that Fellow Freemasons are often easy to recognise, not by externals, but by the persona that they project in their lives, so that symbols are an allegory for the spiritual progress that has taken place in the individual. Elsewhere it has been said that the sign of a Master Mason, that is the real sign, the quality that sets him apart, is in one sense quite obvious to the world at large. Only another (real) Master Mason can recognise the sign for what it is, but its quality shines clearly like a beacon, and almost everyone recognises the person who exhibits it as someone extraordinary.[30]

The five points of fellowship proceed from the signs, and incorporate the mutual support we mentioned earlier. They may also remind you of the charge in the first degree, which mentioned:

'. . . the important duties you owe to God, to your neighbour, and to yourself . . . to your neighbour, by acting with him on the square, by rendering him every kind office which justice or mercy may require, by relieving his necessities and soothing his afflictions, and by doing to him as in similar cases you would wish he would do to you.'

But the five points of fellowship had a yet more intense message, a most compelling and imperative exhortation to exercise your duties to your fellow-men with love and compassion. Your hand shall henceforth be a sure pledge of brotherhood; you will undergo any danger or difficulty in order to offer succour and assistance; your whole attitude shall be one of attention to the needs of others; your heart shall be open to those who need you, closed to those who intend harm to your Brother; your actions and intentions shall be such as will defend your Brother's honour, personal safety and reputation, as well as the honour and safety of those nearest to him.

A third mark

You now left the lodge, and on your return general light had been restored. This signified that your raising to this sublime degree was complete. The former darkness, through which you had to work to discern the greater light, was not now necessary, since you were now in possession of the faculties of a Master Mason, and were able to see clearly with your heart.

The Master once again delegated the Senior Warden to invest you with a new badge, the apron of a Master Mason, to mark the further progress you had made in the science. This science, as you now know, is the science of knowing, the *gnosis* to which we referred, and to which you were now dedicated. And how did this new mark distinguish you? In the previous degree, the apron of a Fellow Craft Freemason was adorned with two rosettes, emblematic of a number of pairs, but chief among them, emblematic of the two pillars at the porchway of King Solomon's Temple. You will recall that the first pillar was but an introduction. The second pillar, in a sense, carried out or executed the properties of the first pillar, and when the two were combined, they formed a whole structure, whole physically and whole spiritually.

Of themselves then, these two pillars appeared to be complete. On the third degree apron however, there is a third rosette, co-ordinating and completing the whole. The new position of the square and compasses on the Volume of the Sacred Law denoted the predominance of the spirit, and therefore implied that mind/body, the first pillar, in conjunction with the soul, the second pillar, are made complete by the Divinity with which you had, so dramatically, become united in this third degree.

The apron was also to:

'. . . *remind you of those great duties you have just solemnly engaged yourself to observe; and whilst it marks your own superiority, it calls on you to afford assistance and instruction to the Brethren in the inferior degrees.*'

Duties. Instruction. The duties are more than the mutual assistance ordained by the five points of fellowship. They imply the duties to yourself in your future life, and through this, your part in the society of which you are a member, to strive for harmony and light, and through that, and by example, to afford assistance and instruction to those who have yet to make the same ascent of Jacob's ladder that you have now made.

Completing the legend

In the traditional history which now followed, we retraced the effects of the loss of the principal architect, Hiram Abiff. The loss referred to here is a cosmic loss. In many legends in many cultures of the world, some ancient cataclysmic tragedy is portrayed: the fall of Man and the expulsion from the Garden of Eden, referred to in the Book of Genesis in the bible, is the one to which we may relate. In that account, through Man's transgression against the law of God, Man lost God's grace and was exiled from paradise, the state of harmony and unity with the Divine. Hiram Abiff's death is of that same order of cosmic tragedy. His murder was a consequence of his fidelity to his fellow-men and the great spiritual intent, the figurative building, which they shared. He died in the pursuit of a higher cause, and his loss therefore is one which affects mankind in general. The secret, the contact with Divinity, was lost, through Hiram's death.

We set out, symbolically, to find the slain Master, but our search at first proves fruitless, because we are looking in the wrong places. The three who do finally find the body are those more enlightened Craftsmen, for they have discerned that the death is indeed the departure of Man from paradise, and to discover that which has died in ourselves, we have only to look into our own hearts. To find the body of the slain Master, we examine and assess our own imperfections, and discover what the third degree teaches us; namely, that if we renounce our transgressions and imperfections, we may attain to the light of a Master Mason. With God's help, we may look beyond the mysterious veil, which we were unable to penetrate with the unaided faculty of reason. As you know, the first two Craftsmen were unable to raise the Master; it needed, as in the case of your own raising, Divine intervention to accomplish the task.

Before we proceed to the third degree tracing board, let us for a moment consider the science of geometry. Geometry is the science of measurement and form; that we may learn to measure ourselves and our actions, to give true and harmonious form to our dealings with others. The second degree lecture calls it 'the first and noblest of sciences', and has an interesting insight which we might well consider here.

'Q.   Why were you passed to the degree of a Fellow Craft?
A.   For the sake of Geometry, or the fifth science on which Masonry is founded.
Q.   Its proper subjects?
A.   Magnitude and extension, or a regular progression of science from a point to a line, from a line to a superficies, and from a superficies to a solid.
Q.   What is a point?
A.   The beginning of geometrical matter.'[31]

109

In other words, the first dimension. Every newly initiated Freemason can be regarded, individually, as a point in space and time. In the above words, he is 'the beginning of geometrical matter', and the lecture quoted establishes the extension of a point to a line, joining us in brotherly love to another Freemason, namely the second dimension, since a line is the shortest distance between two points. The second degree teaches, by the use of the working tools, the use of several lines to enclose a superficial area, namely the third dimension, encompassing a lodge or family. But there is of course a fourth dimension. In an older lecture on the third degree, the question is asked:

'*Q.   From what to what was you raised?*
A.   From a superfice flat to a lively perpendicular; from the square to the compass; from a Fellow Craft to a just and upright Master Mason.'[32]

Now we can begin to see another allegory attached to the word 'raise', and here, in archaic English, we are talking about being 'raised to life', and here is, if we seek it, an echo of the life eternal we spoke of earlier.

A third tracing board

'*Our Master was ordered to be reinterred as near to the Sanctum Sanctorum as the Israelitish law would permit — there in a grave from the centre three feet east and three feet west, three feet between north and south, and five feet or more perpendicular.*'

Clearly, we have here a further allegory, since the exact burial place of Hiram cannot be established by us, nor is its exact geographical location of use to us on our journey.

What is the major import for us of the death of Hiram? Let us look a little further. With his death, as with the expulsion of Adam from the Garden of Eden, Man's bright inner light could not withstand the negative force of Man's transgression, and seemed to be extinguished — the genuine secret was lost, or so it seemed. The full blaze of God's saving and redeeming light was no longer available to

Man. But in the lodge, the glimmering ray was a signal to us, that *God's* light was *not* extinguished, and that by working to retrieve the state of grace that we had lost, we could once again be reunited with that Divine light. At a point deep, deep within ourselves, in a place we may never have visited until now, lies buried the vital and immortal principle which we need to re-discover, our own spirit and spiritual will, a point within the circle of our own nature, our own equivalent of the glimmering ray, and this ray will never be wholly extinguished, no matter how far we may stray from the paths of heavenly science. The grave, then, is ourselves, and the lost guiding light represents our vital and immortal principle, physically delineated by three feet, or an arm's length, in each direction, and five feet or more, our own height, perpendicular, an allegory of our own body. But in its spiritual nature, the vital and immortal principle is that which we may develop, as we developed our sense of moral truth and virtue in the first degree, in order to regain our lost and primal nature, and through that our oneness with God.

Ornaments

'The ornaments of a Master Mason's lodge are the porch, dormer and square pavement.'

We met with lodge ornaments in the first degree, and there the ornaments were the mosaic pavement, the blazing star and the tesselated border round the mosaic pavement. The mosaic pavement you will remember as the black and white chequered floor, pointing out the diversity of objects in the creation, and the blazing star, or glory in the centre, reminded us of the omnipresence of God. You will recall that, in the second degree, you were admitted to the middle chamber of the temple, there to find the name of God, and to receive your spiritual wages. From the middle chamber you have now, in the third degree, progressed to the Sanctum Sanctorum, the holy of holies, and therefore a very special, sacred place.

You entered by the porch, the first of the ornaments here, so this porch is emblematically your transition point from the second to the third degree, just as the door of the middle chamber was your transition point from the first to the second degree. Once we have made that progression, the light of the blazing star becomes the Divine light streaming in through the dormer, the second ornament, lighting up the whole inner space of the Sanctum Sanctorum, and therefore our own inner dimension.

But it is the third ornament, the mosaic pavement, which is common to all three degrees. In the first degree, you stood on the square pavement, and symbolically climbed Jacob's ladder. In the second degree, you were still ascending, now on the winding staircase, leaving the square pavement below. You then progressed through the middle chamber and, in the third degree, you reached the Sanctum Sanctorum, where you stood once again on the square pavement, thus completing the journey coming, as it were, full circle back to the original flooring, although now on a higher plane. In this sense, you yourself are now the ladder, or conscious connection, between the glory, or light through the dormer, and the pavement beneath your feet, and therefore the connection between heaven and earth.

Further tools, co-ordinating

The Master, in this concluding part of the ceremony, presented you with the working tools of a Master Mason. The pencil is the active tool, the skirret is that which constrains the pencil, and the compasses co-ordinate and consolidate the other two. We said that the first degree tools were tools of action, and those of the second degree were tools of testing. Here, the tools are clearly tools of design, of creativity.[33] The pencil delineates, or translates into tangible form, the inner vision of the artist, the creative force. The skirret sets the limits of the pencil, and acts as a measuring agency. The balance or co-ordination between these two is represented by the compasses, which enable the artist 'to ascertain and determine the limits and proportions' of the drawing.

At the completion of the third degree ceremony, let us pause and think for a moment about one of the most important of the architectural implements that has been available to us: the compasses. We spoke of the universality of the square, but of all the implements, whether as great light or as working tool, the compasses comprise an implement which is common to all three degrees. In all three degrees, the compasses were present as the third of the great lights: in the first degree dominated by the square, indicating the persistance of material concerns; in the second degree in shifted perspective, indicating the emergence of the spiritual dimension. In the third degree, where the compasses were fully liberated from the dominance of the square, they were made available to us as the third of the working tools.

Let us further examine the importance of the compasses. In the second degree closing, you will recall the exchange between the Master and the Wardens:

'Master: *Brother Junior Warden, in this position what have you discovered?*
Junior Warden: *A sacred symbol.*
Master: *Brother Senior Warden, where is it situated?*
Senior Warden: *In the centre of the building.*
Master: *To whom does it allude?*
Junior Warden: *The Grand Geometrician of the Universe.'*

This 'centre' refers to God, and is a point from which a Master Mason progresses; it is a starting point for the third degree, for here the compasses are used to place one point on that centre, denoting the Divine presence, and to use the other point to determine the limits we set ourselves. As an Apprentice or as a Fellow Craft, you would not have been qualified to do this, but with the insight and clarity you now achieve through the third degree, you are able, with God as the centre of the lodge, and also the centre or reference point of your Self, to describe the bounds of your life, your duties and your actions. Correct moral conduct is thus defined by boundaries of life and actions which have as their reference point the centre, the place of Divinity within our Self.

But as the compasses are given to us to define both the point and the circumference of the circle round that point, they thus enable us to recognise our duties and our responsibilities in the world. So too the skirret is given to us to exercise a proper restraint in seeing those responsibilities carried out.[34]

There is another aspect of the study of the working tools by which we may profit. The first working tool of the second degree was the square, which as you know, is also the second of the three great lights. In this third degree, the third of the three great lights, the compasses, are made available for our use as the third working tool. In this way, the Craft of Freemasonry successively frees, in the second and third degrees, two of the three great lights, implying that as we gain in spiritual competence, we are at liberty to work with those great lights in the accomplishment of our building.

Opening the lodge in the third degree

You will remember the importance of the password giving you access to the third degree lodge. As you know, there was a need for you to be in harmony and consonance with this new, raised-consciousness lodge so, as before in the second degree, the opening raises the consciousness of the Brethren. By this opening ceremony, they therefore pass from the second degree state, the intellectual or heart knowledge of nature and science, to the higher state, a state in which they achieve oneness with Divinity.

When the Master now knocks, he is answered as before by the Wardens. It is a call to the Brethren to direct themselves towards this higher, spiritual plane. Their energy is about to be focused, but to a degree which you now know as the sublime degree of a Master Mason.

As before, the Master calls in turn on the two Wardens, first to see that the distractions of everything not pertaining to the degree are shut out, then to prove all present as Fellow Crafts. Again, this is not so much to ensure that there are no unentitled persons present, but rather to call the Brethren to attention. The next question by the Master is to the Junior Warden, to confirm that he is a Master Mason, and to ascertain by what instruments he will be proved as such. The Junior Warden replies that he will be proved by the square and compasses, and you will remember that it was 'by the united aid of the square and compasses' that you first sought to be admitted to a Master Mason's lodge. Now the Brethren prove themselves Master Masons, this time by three signs, the third one, as we mentioned earlier, symbolically indicating the centre, the point from which they could not err.

Now the Master and the Wardens have the following exchange:

'Master: *Brother Junior Warden, whence come you?*
Junior Warden: *The east.*
Master: *Brother Senior Warden, whither directing your course?*
Senior Warden: *The west.*
Master: *What inducement have you to leave the east and go to the west?*
Junior Warden: *To seek for that which was lost, which, by your instruction and our own industry, we hope to find.*
Master: *What is that which was lost?*
Senior Warden: *The genuine secrets of a Master Mason.*
Master: *How came they lost?*
Junior Warden: *By the untimely death of our Master, Hiram Abiff.*
Master: *Where do you hope to find them?*
Senior Warden: *With the centre.*
Master: *What is a centre?*
Junior Warden: *A point within a circle, from which every part of the circumference is equidistant.*
Master: *Why with the centre?*
Senior Warden: *That being a point from which a Master Mason cannot err.'*

This bears direct reference to those Craftsmen who were sent out by King Solomon to seek Hiram after he had disappeared, and leaving the temple, the location of light, knowledge and wisdom, proceeded westwards towards the dark, ignorance and death. And we learn that there can be only one reason for such a journey — 'to seek for that which was lost'. Remember what we had to say about the fall of Man and his removal from the light of God. The secrets are called 'genuine' because they are the secrets which are at the origin of Freemasonry, and are the reason why we follow this ancient Craft, namely the search for knowledge of God and of the Self. These then are secrets lost 'by the untimely death of our Master', emblematic of the death of the spirit, or the fall of Man, and they are to be found, we are told, with the centre, that being a point from which we cannot err. Here is enshrined the core, the essence of what it means to be a Freemason, and if we remember that, then our masonic journey will fulfil us.

As soon as the Master declares the Master Mason's lodge open, as in the second degree, three important things happen to confirm the new raised status. The Junior Deacon replaces the second degree tracing board with that of the third degree, the Immediate Past Master rearranges the square and compasses on the Volume of the Sacred Law, and then replaces the working tools of the second degree with those of the third. The lodge and the Brethren are now ready for third-degree labour.

Closing the lodge in the third degree

As you know, the aim of closing is to gently abate the raised energy of this degree. We seek here to close and seal the sensitivity of all present, to close the door which we opened by the act of opening the Master Masons' lodge. The Master, as before, satisfies himself that the lodge is still close tyled. The Brethren then stand to order again, to remind themselves of their special status as Master Masons within the walls of the temple.

The exchange between the Master and the Wardens follows the reverse pattern of that at the opening:

'*Master:*　　　　　*Brother Junior Warden, whence come you?*
Junior Warden:　　*The west, whither we have been in search of the genuine secrets of a Master Mason.*
Master:　　　　　*Brother Senior Warden, have you found them?*
Senior Warden:　　*We have not, Worshipful Master, but we bring with us certain substituted secrets, which we are anxious to impart for your approbation.*'

This seems perplexing, even perverse. Taken at face value, it seems to say that, although you have progressed through this degree, and although you have been raised as a Master Mason, yet the genuine secrets are not there; you must be content with substituted secrets. This is clearly not so; through the ceremony of raising, you have symbolically achieved a state of oneness with Divinity. You have indeed embraced the genuine secret, namely knowledge of God and of the Self. Once you have achieved that state, nothing can ever take it away. This is a puzzle for which, once again, allegories are there to help us. The lesson of this exchange with the Wardens is that, through the restorative and transformative power of God, you have achieved a state of Divine grace, *but this is yours alone*. You cannot communicate it to another, not even a fellow Master Mason. A substituted secret is a verbal symbol, since the true secret is beyond the ability of language to communicate. And the final, p. sign indicates that, as we mentioned earlier, the secret, this state of grace, is to be found, to be experienced, at our own centre.

As in the former degree, the Senior Warden now closes the lodge, the Junior Deacon replaces the second degree tracing board, the Immediate Past Master adjusts the great lights and replaces the second degree working tools. With this, the energy level is once again lowered to that of the second degree.

At one level, it is impossible to sum up here as we did in the other two degrees. We cannot put into words the glory and immensity of what has passed. Just as the name of God was unpronounceable for the ancients, so we find here that words are not enough, and this is as it should be. It is worth while on occasions taking a moment to experience and feel what has gone before, and in that still moment, be with yourself, and know that something remarkable has taken place.

And you should know something further: that this journeying is a continuous process. None of us attains absolute perfection. The object is the striving for it, using allegory, symbol, and above all the insights of the heart. May you, my Brother, continue to be fulfilled, and to grow in knowledge, wisdom, light and love.

Avenues for exploration in the third degree

As in the sections on the first and second degrees, these are only suggestions, and you are encouraged to develop some avenues for exploration of your own.

Meaning of, and need for, the password

Comparison of the square and compasses, and the hexalpha

Application of the Rule of Three to the third degree working tools

Masonic illustrations of birth, life and death

Physical death vis-à-vis figurative death

Aspects of eternity in the third degree

The need for mysteries to be hidden

The need for veils to conceal

Transition, and the function of passwords in the second and third degrees

Personal darkness vis-à-vis general darkness

The glimmering ray

From matter to spirit: from darkness to light

Duties to your neighbour in the first degree vis-à-vis the five points of fellowship

Aspects of the circle and its contents

Different aspects of the contents of the grave

Moral truth, intellectual truth

Regeneration and transformation

Emblems of mortality leading to self-knowledge

Location of the immortal principle

Relation of the morning star to the 'king of terrors'

The square pavement in the first and the third degrees

The 'superiority' of Master Masons over Fellow Crafts and Apprentices

Duties to self vis-à-vis duties to others

Departure from grace: approach to grace

Aspects of geometry in Freemasonry

Power of reason vis-à-vis insights of the heart

Raising: figurative and physical

The point within a circle in the context of the third degree

Application of the Rule of Three to the ornaments of a Master Mason's lodge

Different functions of the two legs of the compasses

East versus west

The centre — location of God, location of the Self

Glossary of terms used in the third degree

This glossary should be used in conjunction with the glossaries at the end of the first and second degree sections.

Allegory	a subject with an underlying meaning as well as the literal one
Apron	an article of dress worn in front of the body, originally to protect from dirt or injury; the principal clothing of a Freemason, and emblem of innocence and of friendship; in the third degree, in altered form from that of the second degree
Aspirant	one who, with steady purpose, seeks advancement, privilege or advantage; a person applying to be initiated into Freemasonry, or to be advanced to a higher degree
Badge	*see* Apron
Beauty	a quality which affords keen pleasure to the senses, or which charms the moral or intellectual faculties; the allegorical name of the third of the three pillars supporting a Freemason's lodge, represented by the pillar of the Corinthian order near to the Junior Warden's pedestal
Blazing Star	the symbol traditionally present in the centre of the lodge, representing God; sometimes also called the Glory, depicted in the third degree by the light streaming in through the dormer (*q.v.*)
Blessing	declaration of Divine favour; benediction
Candidate	*see* Aspirant
Ceremonial	relating to ceremonies or rites; ritual
Ceremony	an outward rite or observance, held sacred. In Craft Freemasonry there are three ceremonies, one for each degree

Circle	a plane figure bounded by a single line, called the circumference, which is everywhere equidistant from a point within it called the centre
Compasses	an instrument for taking measurements and describing circles, used in Freemasonry in an allegorical sense; the third of the three great lights, and the third of the working tools in the third degree
Consciousness	knowledge as to which one has the testimony within oneself
Craft	the practice of speculative Freemasonry
Deacon	name given to the fourth and fifth officers of the lodge. They are messengers; the Senior Deacon communicates between the Master and the Senior Warden, the Junior Deacon between the two Wardens. The Junior Deacon, placed at the right of the Senior Warden in the west, may be regarded as representative of feeling and intuition, and the Senior Deacon, placed at the right of the Master in the east, as representative of awakening. These two officers are responsible for conducting the aspirant during degree ceremonies
Divinity	deity, godhead; the character or quality of the Deity
Dormer	the second of the three ornaments of a Master Mason's lodge; the window that gave light to the Sanctum Sanctorum (q.v.)
Eternal	without beginning or end; that which has always existed and always will exist
Eternity	the quality, condition or fact of being eternal
Fiat	(*Latin:* 'let it be done') a word by which a competent authority sanctions the doing of something, as in 'fiat lux' ('let there be light')

Glory	*see* Blazing Star
Gnosis	knowledge; a special knowledge of spiritual mysteries
God	a superhuman being who is worshipped as having power over nature and the fortunes of mankind
Grace	the Divine influence which operates in men to regenerate and sanctify, and to impart strength to endure trial and resist temptation
Grand Principles	brotherly love, relief and truth, the principles on which Freemasonry is founded
Great Lights	the Volume of the Sacred Law, the compasses and square. In a Freemasons' temple, the great lights are placed on the pedestal of the Master
Hiram Abiff	the principal architect of King Solomon's Temple, responsible for its adornment and beautification. According to the legend in the third degree, he was put to death by those who were determined to obtain the secrets of the third degree by improper means
Holy of Holies	*see* Sanctum Sanctorum
Immortal	not mortal; not subject to death; undying; living for ever
Intellect	perception, discernment, meaning, sense, understanding; that faculty of the mind and heart by which one knows
Jewels	the movable jewels of the lodge are the square, level and plumb rule; the immovable jewels are the tracing board, the rough ashlar and the perfect ashlar
Junior Deacon	*see* Deacon
Junior Warden	*see* Warden
Knowledge	state of being aware or informed; consciousness
Legend	an unauthentic story handed down by tradition

Lodge	an assembly of Freemasons duly warranted by a Grand Lodge
Master Mason	the name given to one who has been raised to the third degree in Freemasonry
Materialism	the doctrine that nothing exists except matter and its movements and modifications; that the phenomena of consciousness and will are wholly due to the operation of material agencies
Moral	of or pertaining to the distinction between right and wrong, or good and evil, in relation to actions, volitions or character
Morning Star	applied to Christ, also to any person who is regarded as the precursor of a figurative 'dawn'
Mortality	the condition of being subject to death; mortal nature or existence
Mosaic pavement	*see* Square pavement
Most High	the name given by Freemasons in the third degree to the Supreme Being; God.
Mystery/mysteries	a hidden or secret thing; something beyond human reason
Obligation	*see* Vow
Ornaments of the lodge	in the third degreee in Freemasonry, the porch, dormer and square pavement
Password	a word given to permit an aspirant to proceed to a degree higher than the one for which he is currently qualified
Pavement	*see* Square pavement
Perambulation	*see* Pilgrimage
Philosophy	the love, study and pursuit of wisdom, or of knowledge of things and their causes
Pilgrimage	a journey to a sacred place as an act of religious devotion. In Freemasonry, the circuit made by the aspirant accompanied by the Deacon, accomplished by passing up the north side of the lodge, across in front of

the Master in the east, down the south side past the Junior Warden, and across in front of the Senior Warden in the west, finishing in front of the Inner Guard. In the third degree there are three pilgrimages: the first two prove the aspirant in the first two degrees, the third proves him as prepared, inwardly and outwardly to be raised to the third degree

Porch — the first of the ornaments of a Master Mason's lodge; the entrance to the Sanctum Sanctorum

Providence — the foreknowing and beneficent care and government of God

Regeneration — the process or fact of being born again spiritually; re-creation or re-formation

Ritual — a prescribed order of performing devotional service

Sanctum Sanctorum — in King Solomon's Temple, the central place, the 'holy of holies' in the west of the temple. The Master Mason's lodge is representative of this very holy place

Self — that which in a person is really and intrinsically she or he; the mind or soul

Senior Deacon — *see* Deacon

Senior Warden — *see* Warden

Soul — the spiritual part of man in contrast to the purely physical

Spirit — the animating or vital principle in man; that which gives life to the physical organism, regarded as originating from God

Square — a building implement for proving an angle of 90 degrees; a four-sided equilateral geometric figure; applied in Freemasonry *inter alia* to test moral conduct

Square pavement — the black and white chequered flooring of the lodge, also the third of the three ornaments of a Master Mason's lodge,

	being the flooring of the Sanctum Sanctorum (*q.v.*)
Sublime	belonging to the highest regions of thought, reality or human activity
Tau cross	a cross of three limbs, i.e. in the shape of a T. It is a symbol of salvation and of consecration, also a symbol of trampling evil underfoot
Third degree	the third of three grades or levels of attainment in Freemasonry, also called the Master's or Master Mason's degree
Tracing Board	normally a wooden board on which are painted or depicted the emblems and symbols of each of the degrees in Freemasonry. A separate design is used in each degree, particular to that degree
Transformation	change in character or condition. In Freemasonry, applied to the spiritual change brought about by the conferral of a degree
Transgression	passing beyond the bounds of legality or right; a violation of law, duty or command; disobedience, trespass or sin
Transition	a passing or passage from one condition or action to another
Truth	that which is consistent with fact or reality; faithful; loyal; in Freemasonry, the third of the three Grand Principles (*q.v.*)
Veil	the piece of precious cloth separating the sanctuary from the body of King Solomon's Temple, figuratively applied by Freemasons to indicate that which separates a Freemason from true knowledge of the Divinity within himself
Vow	an oath of fidelity sworn by a Freemason at his initiation, and subsequently also on his advancement to each of the other two degrees. It is sworn with his hand on the Volume of the Sacred Law

125

Warden	name given to the second and third officers of the lodge. Together with the Master, they are considered the three principal officers. The Senior Warden may be considered representative of the soul of man, the Junior Warden representative of the mind and body. In English lodges, the Senior Warden is placed in the west, directly opposite the Master, and the Junior Warden is placed in the south, equidistant from the Master and the Senior Warden
Wisdom	an understanding of the highest principles of things, that functions as a guide for living a truly exemplary life
Working tools	in the third degree, the skirret, pencil and compasses. Their symbolism is used in a speculative sense

---

[24] Wilmshurst, *The Meaning of Masonry*, page 127
[25] *The Lectures of the Three Degrees in Craft Masonry*
[26] Wilmshurst, *The Meaning of Masonry*, page 125
[27] *The Lectures of the Three Degrees in Craft Masonry*
[28] MacNulty, *The Way of the Craftsman*, page 137
[29] Dyer, *Symbolism in Craft Freemasonry*, page 109
[30] MacNulty, *The Way of the Craftsman*, page 131
[31] *The Lectures of the Three Degrees in Craft Masonry*
[32] Dyer, *Symbolism in Craft Freemasonry*, page 140
[33] MacNulty, *The Way of the Craftsman*, page 139
[34] Dyer, *Symbolism in Craft Freemasonry*, page 138

Suggestions for further

reading

Suggestions for further reading

Barker Cryer, Neville, *I Just Didn't Know That*,
  Lewis Masonic, 1999. ISBN 0-85318-219-1
Barker Cryer, Neville, *Did You Know This Too?*,
  Lewis Masonic, 2005. ISBN 0-85318-241-8
Brunton, Paul, *Discover Yourself*,
  Samuel Weiser, 1971. ISBN 0-87728-592-6
Curl, James Stevens, *The Art and Architecture of Freemasonry*,
  Batsford, 1991. ISBN 0-7134-5827-5
Dyer, Colin, *Symbolism in Craft Freemasonry*,
  Lewis Masonic, 1976. ISBN 0-85318-233-7
Haunch, T. O., *Tracing Boards — Their Development and Their
  Designers*, Quatuor Coronati, 1963. ISBN 0-907655-95-5
Lennhoff, Eugen, *The Freemasons*,
  Lewis Masonic, 1978. ISBN 0-85318-111-X
MacNulty, W. Kirk, *Freemasonry — A Journey Through Ritual and
  Symbol*, Thames & Hudson, 1991. ISBN 0-500-81037-0
MacNulty, W. Kirk, *The Way of the Craftsman*,
  Central Regalia, 2002. ISBN 0-954-2516-0-1
The Lectures of the Three Degrees in Craft Masonry,
  Lewis Masonic
The Way of Hermes, transl. Clement Salaman *et al.*,
  Gerald Duckworth, 1999. ISBN 0-7156-3093-8_
Ward, J. S. M., *An Interpretation of our Masonic Symbols*,
  London, A. Lewis, 1956
Wilmshurst, W. L., *The Meaning of Masonry*,
  Kessinger Publishing, 1993. ISBN 1-56459-373-8